MARLON
BRANDO

MARLON BRANDO

DAVID DOWNING

STEIN AND DAY/*Publishers*/New York

First published in the United States of America in 1984
Copyright © 1984 by David Downing
All rights reserved, Stein and Day, Incorporated
Printed in the United States of America
STEIN AND DAY/*Publishers*
Scarborough House
Briarcliff Manor, N.Y. 10510

Library of Congress Cataloging in Publication Data

Downing, David.
  Marlon Brando.

  Filmography: p.
  Includes index.
  1. Brando, Marlon.   2. Actors—United States—
Biography.   I. Title.
PN2287.B683D68   1984   791.43′028′0924   [B]   84-40244
ISBN 0-8128-2981-6

Acknowledgements

The author and publishers would like to
thank the following for the use of
photographs included in this volume:
Page 10: Universal
Pages 137, 173, 176–77, 181: United Artists
Pages 188, 194: Omni Zoetrope
All remaining photographs courtesy of
The Kobal Collection

CONTENTS

PART 1
A BRUTE OF AN ANGEL

"BUD"

1924 WAS something of a watershed year. The nuclear physicist Werner Heisenberg was busy studying the behavior of sub-atomic particles, and deducing from this study his famous principle, that the only sure thing in life was uncertainty. News of this discovery had not yet reached Hollywood and, indeed, it's doubtful whether it ever reached Cecil B. DeMille, then engaged in putting the finishing touches to his first version of *The Ten Commandments*.

The nascent superstar, complete with chaps

This film offered an approach to the realities of life on a single planet which typified much of Hollywood's product in the inter-war years: it had lots of action, lots of moralizing, an army of poorly-paid extras, and it proved beyond doubt that a resolute application of American know-how and values could part the Red Sea.

Unbeknownst to DeMille or Hollywood the future champion of a more thoughtful American cinema was being born that year in Omaha, Nebraska. On April 3, Marlon and Dorothy Brando welcomed the arrival of their third child and first son, Marlon Jr.

Omaha was hardly an auspicious birthplace for a revolutionary, and at least one of the two parents involved would have found such a thought profoundly distasteful. Marlon Sr. was a solid, conservative mid-westerner who made his living in agricultural

The family exchanges pleasantries. Brando with mother and sister

products, spending a fair proportion of his time away from home retailing the company wares. He was more than a farm-to-farm salesman though; the Brandos were prosperous enough to employ servants, and Marlon Sr. himself was respected as a minor pillar of Omaha society.

His wife, on the other hand, was far from a conservative, at least insofar as Omaha society was concerned. Dorothy Pennebaker Brando, or "Dodie" as she was universally known, read the latest literature, painted and sculpted, and actively promoted the city's Community Playhouse Theater. The Brando home was often overflowing with those elements of higher society which the more staid liked to term Bohemian.

This apparently odd couple seem, during the twenties, to have been a fortunate one, with each partner happily pursuing divergent interests within a framework of domestic harmony. The three children—Jocelyn (born 1921), Frances (1922) and young "Bud"—enjoyed a home life that was both stable and interestingly different. But as the decade drew to a close, and their nation entered the very different world of the thirties, the Brandos were just one more family to feel the chill of the winds shaking the fabric of American society. Marlon Sr.'s business interests dictated a move to Evanston, a rural suburb of Chicago, and all Dodie's cultural involvement in Omaha had to go by the board. Two more moves followed in the next few years, first to California, then back to Illinois and another rural suburb, Libertyville. They still lived a life of relative affluence—their home was an eight-acre farm—but the moves had somehow disrupted the balance of the marital relationship. Marlon Sr. was not moving up in the world as fast as he'd expected, and Dodie had to be content with day-trips to Chicago for her cultural refuelling. Perhaps their personal disappointments infected the marriage, perhaps it was simply the passing of the years, but they began to drift apart, and Dodie drifted into an intermittent alcoholism.

The effect of all this on the growing children is impossible to gauge, but Marlon Jr., the youngest, was probably the one most deeply affected. He was noted for his energy, his competitiveness, his general refusal to conform, and his intuitive feeling for the underdog. He brought home wounded animals and, in at least one instance, a "wounded" person. At school he was considered as bright as he was irresponsible. He never acted in any of the school plays—the detention class had already claimed his presence.

This general attitude struck no chords in his father, and his mother, who might have recognized her own leaning in her son's youthful iconoclasm, was drawing more and more away from the family and into herself. At the age of seventeen Bud was dispatched by his father to the Shattuck Military Academy in Farbault, Minnesota. Perhaps a sustained dose of military discipline would bring the boy to his "senses."

Of course it did no such thing: Shattuck seems only to have confirmed young Marlon in his anarchistic instincts. After eighteen months of inner resentment and outward rebellion he was ingloriously expelled, allegedly for smoking, though other, more spectacular versions of the event were to be offered in later years. While at the academy, Marlon had damaged a knee playing football, and this rendered him ineligible for the war now consuming half the globe. He returned home to a despairing father, an unreachable mother and a job laying drainage tiles. His friends had all gone off to war. He was nineteen years old, trained for nothing, ready for nothing, lacking any coherent vision of his own future.

NEW YORK

One thing he knew—he had to get away from home. His choices were somewhat limited by lack of money, but sister Frances was in New York, studying art, and her Greenwich Village apartment offered a useful first stop. Like other mid-westerners arriving in the city for the first time—"everything was so big I couldn't see the sky" one Bob Dylan would later recall—Brando found New York instantly captivating. This was the melting-pot, the place where Europe and America met, the place where things happened. He

went through a succession of jobs, driving a truck, selling lemonade on the sidewalk, taking an elevator up and down in a big department store. And he absorbed the extraordinary vitality of the city, its myriad sights, smells, accents, a world in microcosm.

On the other end of the telephone line to Libertyville his father was still asking pertinently irritating questions like, "What are you going to do with your life?" and "When are you going to do it?" His other sister, Jocelyn, was learning to act at the New School for Social Research, and she seemed to be having a great deal of fun. Why not become an actor, at least for a while? It would please his mother, halt the flow of parental frustration emanating from his father. If he didn't like it he could always try something else.

He swiftly made his mark. It took only a week for Stella Adler, who ran the New School, to decide that "within a year Marlon Brando will be the best young actor in the American theater." Perhaps Bud had found his metier at last.

The School's Dramatic Workshop was run by Erwin Piscator, an Expressionist escapee from Nazi Germany, and it was under his direction that Brando played his first roles: a guard and a giraffe in a play put on for the Children's Theater at the Adelphi. More serious roles followed: an angel and a teacher in a workshop production of Hauptmann's *Hannele's Way to Heaven,* Sebastian in *Twelfth Night,* a variety of parts in a series of Molière plays. He was noticed by both the critics ("a promising newcomer" etc.) and the thronging agents in search of future meal-tickets.

But the undisciplined Bud hadn't disappeared. In the summer of 1944 Piscator led his students to Long Island for a season of performances in front of paying audiences, and the young Brando, discovered in bed with one of the actresses, was sent home in disgrace like an errant boy scout. This "promising newcomer" was not going to play it the easy way.

Back in New York his mother had arrived to set up home for her three children, and for a time the arrangement seems to have suited all concerned. Marlon was offered a part in a production of John Van Druten's *I Remember Mama,* and the family went through the script together. It was so riveting that they all fell asleep. But Stella Adler thought the play would be a hit, and advised Brando to accept the part of sixteen-year-old Nels. No matter how bad the play was in artistic terms, a success in commercial terms would undoubtedly get him useful publicity. He took the part.

I Remember Mama, one of the few Norwegian-American soap operas in recorded history, opened in October 1944 and was indeed a hit, running for over 700 performances and eventually winning the ultimate soap opera accolade, transformation into a TV series. Nels, as Brando said, was "not a showy part . . . there was nothing more I could do with it." But still the reviewers managed to pick him out; there was something special about this beautiful boy, some hint of electricity in his acting.

He was still at the New School, taking courses in psychology, French and History of Art. In his spare time he read Kant, Plato, Schopenhauer, Kafka and other authors who hadn't yet made it big in the mid-west. And, most important of all, he moved on to Stella Adler's class in "Method" acting, little knowing that one day his own name would be virtually synonymous with everything that "Method" came to stand for in the public mind.

The original "Method" approach had been developed forty years before and many miles away, by Konstantin Stanislavsky, during his work with the Moscow Art Theater. It was and is difficult to define, but it centered on the projection of inner emotional experience through controlled improvization by both actors and directors. It arrived in America in the twenties, and its apparent left-wing credentials found favor with that part of the American theatrical establishment which viewed the Great Depression as more of a human tragedy than a commercial hiccup. The Group Theater, formed at the beginning of the thirties, and featuring such illustrious names as Harold Clurman, Lee Strasberg and Elia Kazan, adopted Stanislavsky's teachings with enthusiasm, and applied them to great effect in their production of plays like Odets' *Waiting for Lefty.* For them "Method" was akin to realism and realism was akin to a highly critical view of American social reality. It had rebellion written into it.

The Group Theater broke up on the eve of war, but many of its prominent luminaries went on to great individual success with both plays and films. The most notable of these was Elia Kazan, the son of Greeks from Istanbul who'd arrived in the States at the beginning of the century. Kazan had studied costume, lighting, scenery and production at drama school, written one-act plays, joined both the Group Theater and, briefly, the American Communist Party in the early thirties. Gradually he worked his way into direction, and when the Group Theater disbanded, he struck out on his own with great success, scoring several smash hits on Broadway with plays that, unusually for the time, dealt with contemporary social issues.

Early in 1946 he and Clurman were putting together a production of Maxwell Anderson's *Truckline Cafe,* a play which gathered several individual stories into the one fictional post-war location. Clurman was to direct, he happened to be Stella Adler's husband, and she happened to have this young actor for one of the parts. So Brando played McRae, a soldier returning from the war to confront and kill his unfaithful wife. It was a short part but a demanding one. Brando had to arrive onstage drenched, exhausted and shivering, and to get this effect he would run up and down the lighting stairs backstage, have two buckets of water hurled at him, and then stagger out into the spotlight at the appropriate moment, there to tell the story of his wife's unfortunate demise. A quarter of a century later, reviewing *Last Tango in Paris,* Paulene Kael recalled one of his performances: "I looked up and saw what I thought was an actor having a seizure onstage. Embarrassed for him, I lowered my eyes, and it wasn't until the young man who'd brought me grabbed my arm and said, "Watch this guy!" that I realized he was *acting.*"

The play didn't last long—Clurman and Kazan wanted revisions which the writer refused to contemplate—but Brando's notable performances assured him of more work. According to some stories, he was offered a screentest by Twentieth Century-Fox around this time, but, turning up on the chosen day with a yoyo and little apparent enthusiasm, failed to impress the movie-men. According to other stories—all of Brando's early career is shrouded in rumor, invention and unreliable hearsay—the actor himself was extremely reluctant to enter the contract-ridden world of movies, and offer after offer was turned down. Yet more stories claim that

Brando talks with Elia Kazan on the set of *A Streetcar Named Desire* the unwillingness was the studio's, not Brando's. They had all the celluloid heroes they needed, without importing new and probably troublesome young actors from Broadway.

Whatever the truth of the matter, Brando stayed with the stage. *Candida* was his next play, the poet Eugene Marchbanks his next role. It was a considerable jump for the actor, from the naturalism of the modern, "methodistic" theater to Shaw's stylized classic, and opinions differed as to how well he'd managed it. Marchbanks was a notoriously difficult role to play, and he was following in some rather large footsteps, Orson Welles' and Burgess Meredith's to name but four.

Fortunately, perhaps, the production only lasted a few weeks,

and Brando was quickly signed up for another contemporary piece, *A Flag Is Born*. As the title and the time suggest, this play centered around the ongoing struggle for a Jewish homeland in Palestine, and it worked rather better as propaganda than as drama. Brando had accepted the role in part because his sympathies were engaged in the real-life drama, in part because he was eager to work with the famous Paul Muni.

The Flag was furled after 127 performances, and his career took another half-somersault, landing him in Cocteau's *The Eagle has Two Heads* and under the matriarchal gleam of the legendary Tallulah Bankhead. The two did not get on—rumor had it that Tallulah disliked both being rejected and being up-staged—and Brando was sacked before the play reached New York and a well-deserved panning. It was his first real setback since the trouble with Piscator on Long Island, but it can't have worried him too greatly.

He had moved out of the family apartment by this time, and into one shared with his old schoolfriend Wally Cox and a pet raccoon. It wasn't a palace, and the two young men made no effort to make it one, contenting themselves with painting a small portion of one wall. Brando, for all his recent success, seemed to have changed remarkably little since his arrival in the big city. His idea of a gourmet meal was still a trip to the local hamburger joint, his ideal woman the New York equivalent of the girl next door. He had next to no possessions, didn't drink, took no drugs.

He was just an ordinary lad, too ordinary in fact. He not only played down his success, he even, according to some, went out of his way to avoid anyone who could help him in his career. He seemed to want to avoid stardom, and the reasons for his reluctance would haunt him long after he became a star. On the one hand there was something enduringly immature about him, something that ran away from the responsibilities and restrictions which success implied; on the other there was the man who already knew that the success on offer was ultimately meaningless, that the values behind it were manufactured, false.

It was perhaps this inner ambivalence which made him so perfect for the part which would shoot him to stardom. Stanley Kowalski,

Brando in 1950,
T-shirt to the
fore

for all his un-Brando-like vulgarity and brutality, was also half-innocent, half-knowing.

KOWALSKI

A Streetcar Named Desire was written by the Mississippi-born, thirty-five-year-old Tennessee Williams. He had had one flop with *Battle of Angels* in 1940, and a huge success four years later with *The Glass Menagerie. Streetcar* was to be produced by Irene Mayer Selznick, and she wanted stage and screen star John Garfield for the part of Kowalski.

Garfield wasn't sure about the role. It seemed too subservient to the leading female role, and he demanded that Williams adjust the balance. He also refused to sign a contract exceeding four weeks in duration. Williams said no to the re-write, Selznick said no to the contract, and Garfield was out. The producers turned next to Burt Lancaster, but he was tied up in movie work. Then Kazan, who'd been hired to direct, suggested the part to Brando, whose initial reaction was negative. It was too big a part, too much of a challenge. The character was too far removed from himself or his experience of life. But Kazan persuaded him to talk with Tennessee Williams, and the latter was more than impressed by Brando's reading of the part. The actor held his breath and said yes. It was probably the single most important decision of his career.

Looking back from the heights (or depths) of the eighties, it's not so easy to understand what all the fuss over *Streetcar* was about. But there's no doubt that in 1947 the most common reaction to the play was simple shock. It was so real, so sexually charged, so class-conscious, it touched parts of the body and soul which other contemporary plays just couldn't reach. "It was awful and it was sublime," one critic observed, "only once in a generation do you see such a thing in the theater."

The two central characters were flag-carriers for ways of life. On one side stood the virile, sweaty, iconoclastic Kowalski, summed up by his opponent in one of the play's most quoted speeches: "He acts like an animal, has an animal's habits! Easts like one, moves like one, talks like one! Thousands and thousands of years have passed him right by, and there he is—Stanley Kowalski—survivor of the Stone Age!" All of which was true, but only half the truth. His creator, Williams, stressed the positive side of the character: "Animal joy in his being is implicit in all his movements and attitudes. Since early manhood the center of his life has been pleasure with women . . . with the power and pride of a richly feathered male bird among hens. Branching out from this complete and satisfying center are all the auxiliary channels of his life, such as his heartiness with men, his appreciation of rough humor, his love of good food and drink and games, his car, his radio, everything that is his, that bears his emblem of the gaudy seed-bearer."

Ranged against this "animal" is his wife's sister Blanche, who's come to live with them after being (unknown to the Kowalskis) thrown out of her home town. On the surface she's gentility, culture, the human at the heart of the animal, and at this level she reacts to Kowalski in the manner already quoted. But there's an animal in her too, and she's irresistibly drawn, against all her reason, to him and what he represents. From his side there's resentment: her pretensions are a destabilizing influence in his happy nest.

The play doesn't take sides in the conflict, and indeed some reviewers of the subsequent film bemoaned this lack of a "secure moral center." But according to Kazan this was the whole point, this was what made the story so special. Talking about the movie, he described it as "the first non-sentimental picture we have ever made over here. It is a landmark. Its issues are not over-simplified, and you're not in there "rooting for somebody"—all that old shit the motion picture industry is built upon. There is no hero, no heroine; the people are people, some dross, some gold, with faults and virtues—and for a while you are muddled about them, the way you would be in life."

But if *Streetcar* was a landmark in the theater and in films, it was also a turning-point in acting and the career of one actor. Brando simply astonished audiences with the virtuosity, the sheer nerve-biting intensity of his performances. The actress Shelley Winters, who knew Brando, went to see the play near the beginning of its two-year run: "There was an electrical charge and almost an animal scent he projected over the footlights that made it impossible for the audience to think or watch the other performers on the stage. All you could so was feel, the sexual arousal was so complete. I don't believe this quality can be learned; it's just there, primitive and compelling. The only other time I experienced it was when I saw Elvis Presley perform live in Las Vegas . . ."

But if they thought they were being upstaged, his fellow performers had no grudge. Kim Hunter, who played Stella Kowalski in both play and film, found that Brando had "an uncanny sense of truth. It seems absolutely impossible for him to be false. It makes him easier to act with than anybody else ever. Anything you do that may not be true shows up immediately as false with him."

HOLLYWOOD

"Method," though born in the theater, was to reach its highest fulfillment on the movie screen. Kazan noted that many of the elements of the "Method" approach—the actor's concentration on what the character wants, on what has happened fictionally before the scene he's actually playing—"are cinematic in that they take the reliance off the dialogue, off the spoken word, and put it in activity, inner activity, desire, objects, partners—partners being the people you play with . . ." In the theater, where words mattered most, an actor like Brando could project tremendous presence but not the depth of character of which he was capable. He acted with his eyes, his hands, his body, as well as his voice. The camera could capture for cinema audiences what only the first few rows of a theater audience could hope to see.

Learning to live again. With Teresa Wright in *The Men*

Overleaf: An angry young Wilozek in *The Men*

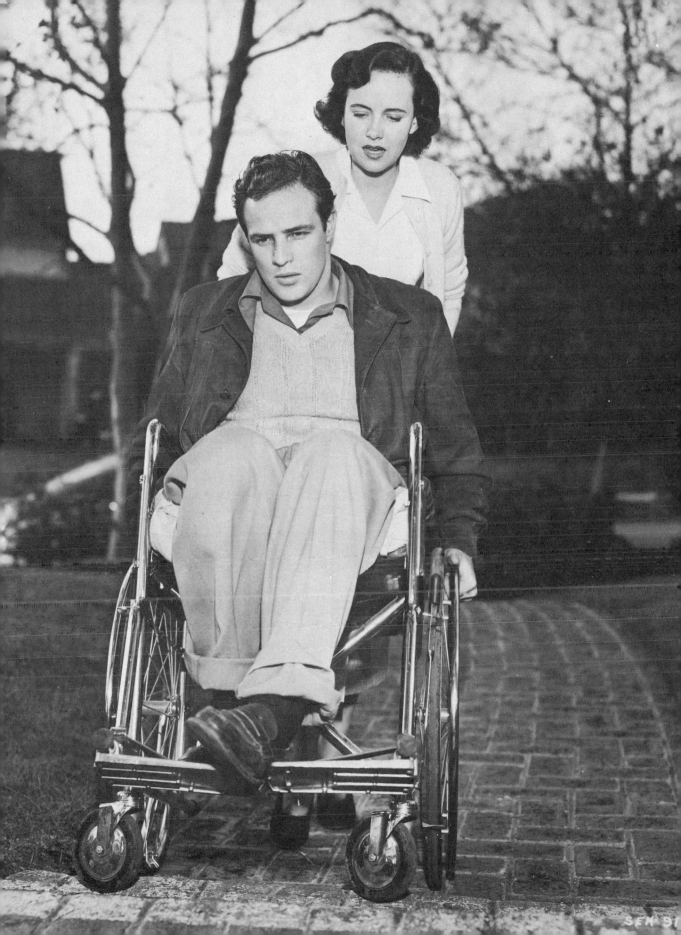

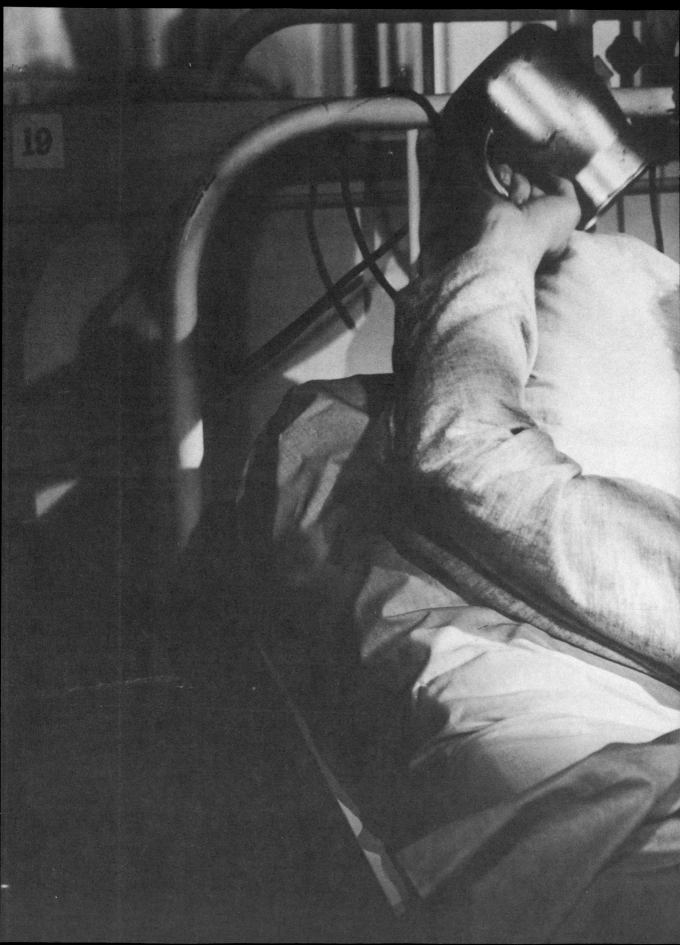

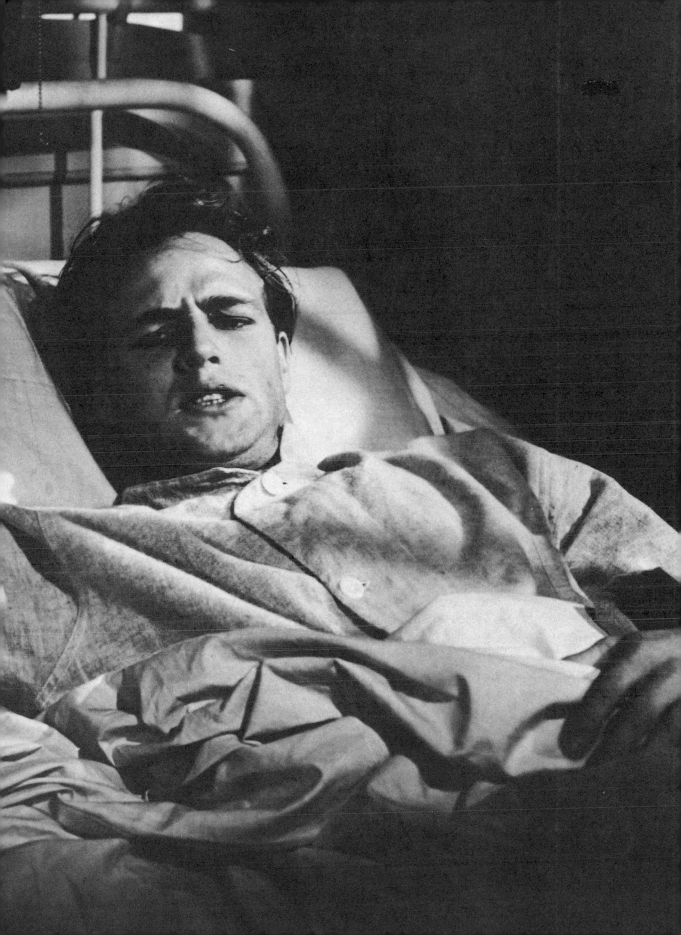

And there were other, less exalted reasons for making the transition. As the *Streetcar* run lengthened into its second year the burden of playing Kowalski day in and day out began to take its toll. He got bored with the play, bored with the character, and increasingly exasperated with being treated offstage as if he really was Kowalski. The $550 a week, which had looked so generous at the start, seemed worth every cent by the time his eighteen-month stint was drawing to a close. It was surely time for something new.

But, then again, Brando had heard a lot of horror stories about Hollywood, and he was in no hurry to become the "property" of a major studio. He didn't like the movie industry's product much, finding Hollywood's world-view "ugly, harmful and distorted." Movies might be "the most powerful single influence available to the American public," but so far as America was concerned that potential was far from being realized. French films, he thought, were "so much more mature and sensitive," not "removed from all reality, as ours are. I just feel dead inside, coming away from most Hollywood screenings." Brando would only embrace the American movie industry on his own terms, as a free agent with a mission to improve the product.

After his run in *Streetcar* ended he took a European holiday, visited museums, sat in bars, met women and read the theater and movie scripts forwarded to him by his agents, MCA. One of the latter interested him, as much for its source as its intrinsic worth. Independent producer Stanley Kramer then had a reputation for making movies which dealt in controversial themes; his last two had been *Champion,* a remarkably unsentimental story of a prizefighter, and *Home of the Brave,* which delved into racism in the U.S. Army. The script for *The Men,* which he'd sent to Brando, was just as socially conscious; it dealt with the paraplegic victims of war.

It seemed the ideal entry into Hollywood: working with an independent producer there'd be no lasting strings, and the subject matter offered, as he said himself, "an important dramatic situation." Director Fred Zinnemann and scriptwriter Carl Foreman both had high reputations. Brando signed to make the film for a $40,000 fee.

But something inside him was still unsure. His distrust of the system, his dislike of Hollywood values, and probably his New York theater sense of superiority, all came tumbling out the moment he reached the celluloid capital. "The only reason I'm here is because I don't yet have the moral strength to turn down the money," he said. Hollywood was "a cultural boneyard," producers had "the manners of ants at a picnic." The accuracy of these observations was largely beside the point; Brando was keeping a distance between himself and the ravening beast of commercial cinema, announcing that their relationship would never be an easy one. He would not be reduced to a mere star.

At work, he was as professional as ever. Since he was playing a paraplegic he would find out what it was like to live as one, and to this end spent almost a month living in a veterans' hospital, traveling, when necessary, by wheelchair. When the shooting started he discovered that movie-acting offered a distinctly new challenge: "It's the toughest form of acting, and anyone who can come through it successfully can call himself an actor for the first time. When you have to portray a shattering emotion while realizing at the back of your mind that if you move your head an inch too much you'll be out of focus and out of frame, that's acting."

The Men concerns two people's reaction to the crippling of one. Ken Wilozek (Brando) is first seen being shot in battle, and for the rest of the film his attempts to reconcile himself with life as a permanent cripple are intertwined with the doubts his condition sows in his relationship with fiancé Ellen (Teresa Wright). At first he refuses to see her—how could she marry him now?—but when he does eventually sum up the courage to envisage a future with her, she, aided and abetted by her family, begins to have her own doubts. They do get married, but on their wedding night all the pent-up anxieties come pouring out in a torrent of hatred. He returns to the hospital only to be discharged; the doctor believes that making the marriage work is his only possible salvation. There is no happy ending, merely an affirmation that the search for one is worth the effort.

It's worth noting at this point that the original story involved

Ellen being tempted by another suitor, one sounder of body, and that the actor hired to play this part was both talentless and the chief financial backer's son. He could not be replaced, so he ended up on the cutting-room floor with a large proportion of Teresa Wright's part. As a result the finished product seems slightly uneven; Ellen is not as real as Ken. The film still worked, but the whole idiotic charade must have served to confirm Brando's existing prejudices about Hollywood.

For the moment he was probably satisfied with his film debut. The movie was praised, despite the unfortunate coincidence of its opening and the onset of the Korean War. Richard Winnington, writing in *Sight and Sound*, thought *The Men* was marked "by the sort of courage we had ceased to expect from English-speaking movies," and generally-speaking reviewers on both sides of the Atlantic were highly respectful. Brando got most of the attention of course, and Hollywood's new *enfant terrible* won universal praise. Winnington thought his "combination of style, depth and range" had come "like a blood transfusion into cinema acting," and Otis Guernsey explained why in the *New York Herald Tribune*. Brando's performance, unlike the normal Hollywood performance, depended "not at all on personality but entirely on the understanding of character and technical virtuosity." *Time* noted that Brando's "halting, mumbled delivery, glowering silences and expert simulation of paraplegics do not suggest acting at all; they look chillingly like the real thing."

TWO WITH KAZAN

Back in New York, Brando reoccupied his one-room apartment and enrolled in several more courses at the New School. He had agreed to do some publicity for the film, but with little enthusiasm. The level of satisfaction he derived from talking about his career

The slob and his dinner. With Kim Hunter in *A Streetcar Named Desire*

Overleaf: Kim Hunter passes on her knitting technique on the set of *A Streetcar Named Desire*

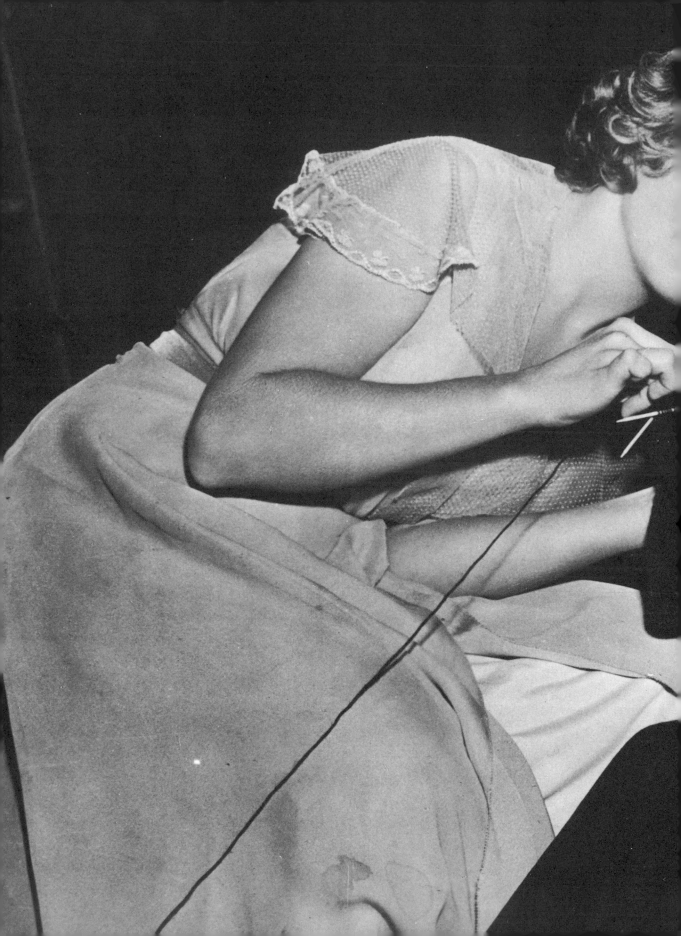

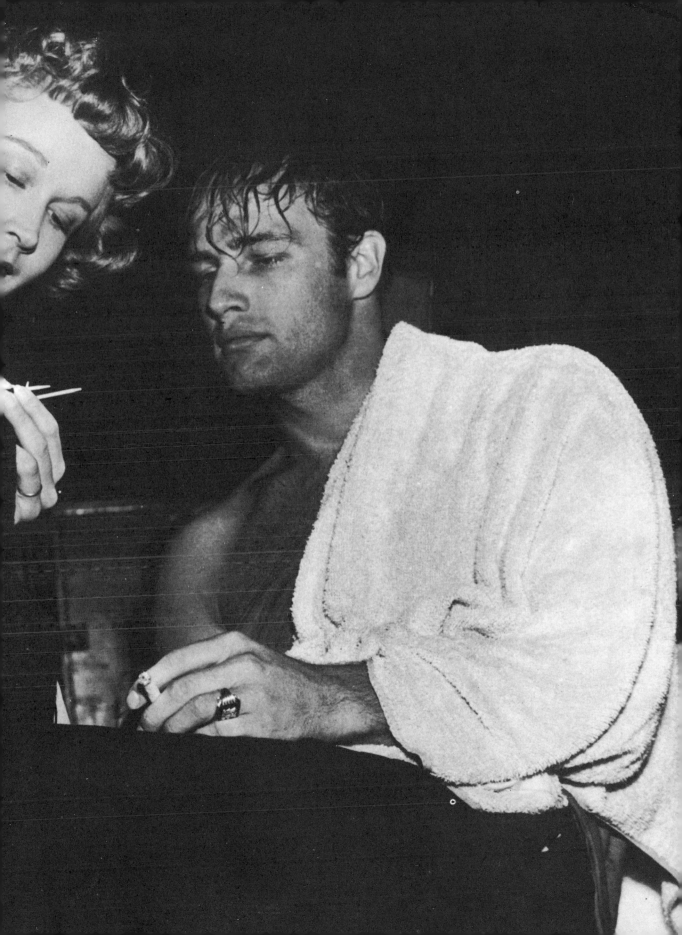

was evident on one chat-show—he fell asleep half way through it.

The next film was to be the cinematic *Streetcar*, with Kazan directing most of the original Broadway cast. Only Jessica Tandy was missing; the studio presumably decided they needed a bigger name, and Vivien Leigh was brought in to recreate the Blanche she'd played in London under husband Olivier's direction.

Kazan and Williams toyed with ways of opening the play out for the movies, but found the difficulties inherent in this approach too much, and settled for virtually filming the stage version. Or would have done so but for the censors. The current production code stated that "adultery and rape, sometimes necessary plot material, must not be explicitly treated, or justified, or presented attractively . . . Excessive and lustful kissing, lustful embraces, suggestive postures and gestures, are not to be shown . . . seduction and rape should never be more than suggested and only then when essential to the plot." All of which made a play like *Streetcar* seem almost hardcore. Changes had to be made, "bad language" excised, references to homosexuality erased. The rape, though left in, was used to punish Stanley. Even the music was made "less carnal."

But, despite all this, the flavor of the original was retained. The *Streetcar* film still seemed daringly original when compared to the mass of the Hollywood product, was still pointed enough to represent a clear breakthrough in the cinema's depiction of human reality. The Brando that had electrified Broadway, even shorn of his "bad language," could still electrify cinema audiences around the world. He was nominated for that year's Academy Award, as he would be in each of the succeeding three years.

When he lost in 1952 to Humphrey Bogart—whose performance in *The African Queen,* though excellent, was hardly revolutionary —there was more than a suspicion of relief in traditionalist Hollywood circles. The young upstart had been taken down a peg! That would give him something to mumble about! Of course, Brando had largely brought this reaction on himself; his talent—if that is the word—for making himself popular with the powers-that-be was underdeveloped to the point of invisibility. He seemed determined to play the outsider as flamboyantly as possible, and though his exploits were often hilarious they were also accurately

The famous torn T-shirt. With Kim Hunter in *A Streetcar Named Desire*

Overleaf: The hero learns to read. With Jean Peters in *Viva Zapata*

interpreted as deliberate affronts to the status quo. Driving down Hollywood Boulevard with a fake arrow stuck through his head was simply amusing, and refusing to accept the gossip-writers on their own self-important terms was doubtless admired by many who wished they shared his nerve, but his refusal to answer the usual banal questions with anything other than insolent put-ons only encouraged the rumor-mongers, and his general disdain for conventions was haughtily resented by those who'd accepted them, however reluctantly. Brando's T-shirt and jeans were seen as a comment on their suits, his answer to the question "how do you best like to bathe?"—"by spitting in the air and running under it"—as an assault on the whole phoney publicity machine.

There were only two alternatives of course. He could either lie back and submit to the machine or he could continue doing what he was doing. But his refusal to submit did exact a price: he was typed as the "slob," the mumbler, his fall from such grace was eagerly awaited. If he ever faltered the Hollywood air would be thick with the flash of knives.

There was no sign of faltering yet. His third film, also directed by Kazan, was *Viva Zapata!,* an epic biographical treatment of the famous Mexican revolutionary. It was an interesting subject in itself, and one with particular relevance to the then-current American political situation. The McCarthy red scare was looming, and placing much of the American Left in something of a political quandary. People like Kazan and friend/screenwriter John Steinbeck seemed to feel the need to distance themselves from both the "hard Left" and the red-baiters. Zapata was an ideal subject because he represented a political position that was both revolutionary and anti-authoritarian, and because his life reflected the basic problem inherent in such a position, the reconciling of socialism and democracy.

The Mexican probably appealed to Brando for much the same political reasons, but initially he was doubtful about playing him. Brando himself was a young, reflective, middle-class American; could he be convincing as an evangelical Mexican peasant who aged twenty years in the course of the story? Kazan convinced him that he could, and with typical thoroughness the actor lived in a

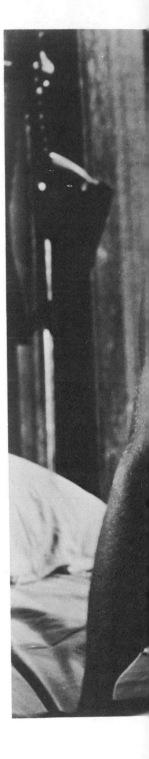

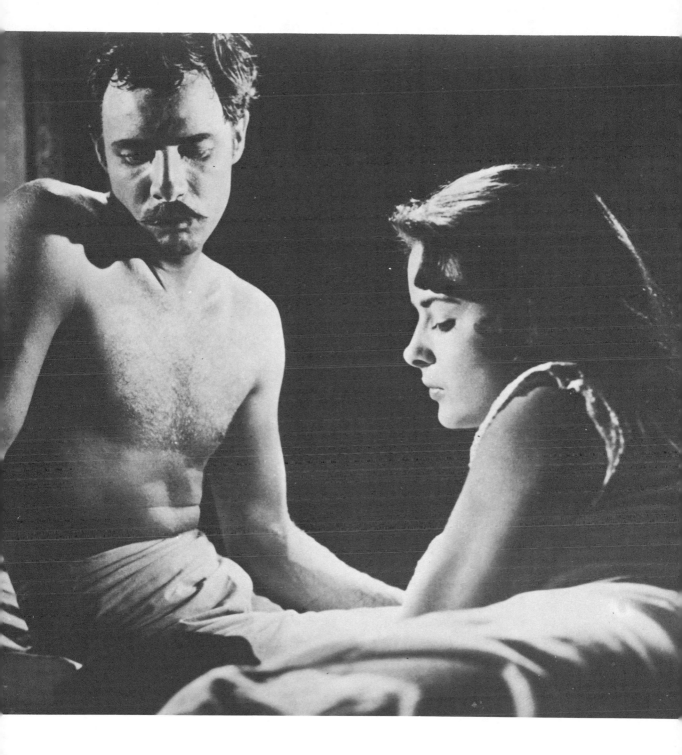

Sonora village for several weeks, studying the local culture and devising his own make-up. It was, after all, a chance to escape the image of the modern "slob."

The story was devised in three parts. In the first the film follows Zapata's sense of injustice through civil war to the triumph of the revolution, in the second his exposure to the insidious corruption of power, in the third his "abdication," self-purification and death. The first and third parts are suitably stirring, the central section rather too predictable. Power corrupts, the film-makers insist, but that's about as far into the situation as they go. The message is pushed home so hard that you begin to wonder whether the fight against injustice can ever be worth pursuing.

The best scenes tend to be the wordless ones, where Kazan's camerawork, the epic settings and Brando's acting provide relief from the self-consciously poetic dialogue of the other scenes. For a Hollywood movie it was, and is, a revolutionary statement of sorts, and Kazan could claim with justification that not since Eisenstein had such a well-meaning epic been put on the screen. But, and it's a big but, the film is as notable for what it leaves out as for what it shows. The sentiments are more epic than the action, which gives little clue to the scale of blood-letting which actually occurred. The economic issues—particularly the land question—are virtually ignored after the first fifteen minutes, as the film firmly focuses on those political issues of democracy and dictatorship more germane to the North American consciousness. Zapata becomes more important than Mexico, political principles more important than mere people.

Twenty years later the Italian director Sergio Leone would cover much the same ground in *Duck, You Sucker* (UK: *A Fistful of Dynamite*), and a comparison of the two films is interesting. Leone's lacks the tragic grandeur which Kazan and Brando bring to theirs, but tragic grandeur is essentially an outsider's appreciation; revolutions are only "grand" in retrospect. In *Duck, You Sucker* Rod Steiger plays a dirty, vulgar, self-seeking peasant who is sucked into the revolutionary struggle against his better judgement. He's real. When tragedy strikes him it feels like tragedy. When people argue about principles in this film there is a

Previous page: Power corrupts, Hollywood-style. With Anthony Quinn, Lou Gilbert and Harold Gordon in *Viva Zapata*

An actor's life. Learning Shakespeare on the set of *Julius Caesar*

connection between the people, the principles and the situation, the theories seem to come out of the human drama. Leone's revolution shows both how low humanity can sink and how high it can soar.

By contrast, Kazan and Steinbeck's revolution is a cowboy story staggering along under the weight of one political idea, and not a very profound one at that. Brando is eminently watchable, much better than the part he's been given, but even he can't escape the one-dimensionality of the Zapata Steinbeck has written; all the conflicts are outside him and there's nothing much for the actor to do. We're left with a magnetic presence and nothing more.

ANCIENT AND MODERN

The days of angling for film offers were now long gone; they poured into MCA, particularly after his second Oscar nomination. Brando was attracted by the idea of working in Europe, but he turned down starring roles in Autant-Laurant's *Stazione Termini* and Zinnemann's projected biography of Van Gogh. Instead he picked on England's most famous author and the role of Mark Antony in a strictly Hollywood version of *Julius Caesar*. Perhaps it was the implicit challenge which appealed to him, perhaps he saw it as an ideal opportunity to ditch the persistent ghost of Kowalski.

The film was the brainchild of John Houseman, Orson Welles' old collaborator at the Mercury Theater, and he intended it to be artistic rather than spectacular. This pleased the MGM production chiefs; spectacle was expensive, whereas the needs of art could be served by a re-use of the *Quo Vadis* sets. The studio would garner prestige and the immediate financial loss would be minimal.

Unfortunately from the studio's point of view, art did require a certain level of acting ability, and Houseman was allowed to gather a highly distinguished cast. Gielgud and James Mason were brought over from England, Brando, Louis Calhern and Edmund

Friends, Romans, technicians – Hollywood's that way!

O'Brien recruited from nearer home, and a couple of female contract players, Deborah Kerr and Greer Garson, thrown in for good measure. Brando was determined not to be outshone in such illustrious company. He spent weeks listening to recordings of classical actors doing Shakespeare, took enunciation lessons, practiced endlessly. It was worth the effort. When the moment came for shooting the famous "Friends, Romans" speech—throughout rehearsals he had not exceeded a low mumble—his ringing declamation elicited equally ringing applause from everyone on the set.

The speech turned out to be the high-point of the film, as it usually is of the play; from that point on Shakespeare's story seems to lose all dramatic focus. In his two other major scenes Brando successfully conveyed Mark Antony's uneasy blend of nobility and scheming selfishness, and though he himself was "not particularly" satisfied with his performance, the critics were generally approving. Houseman himself wrote that "there is no question in my mind that in natural equipment, temperament and application, he is one of the very great actors of our time."

The actor, however, was not too enamored of the cinema, and over the next few years was to make occasional pronouncements of a permanent return to the stage. The only time he actually did retread the boards was in the summer of 1953, taking a self-picked company on a stock tour of New England, performing Shaw's *Arms and the Man*. The play chosen was significantly noncontemporary: this tour was for fun, not artistic discovery.

Still the movie offers poured in. He was set to do the musical *Pal Joey* with Billy Wilder, but pulled out. He was mentioned in connection with a Fritz Lang-directed *Human Desire* and a projected re-make of *A Star Is Born*. But in the end he accepted another role from Kramer, perhaps out of gratitude, but more probably because the provisionally-titled "The Cyclists' Raid" had something to say about the state of the world.

Or would have, had the censors not decided to take another hand in Brando's career. The story concerned the takeover of a small California town by two motorcycle gangs, and it was based on a real-life chronicled in *Harper*'s magazine by Frank Rooney. The

Would you let your daughter marry this boy? Johnny and the Blind Rebels in *The Wild One*

Blind Rebels Motorcycle Club, led by Johnny (Brando), are moved on from one town but stop in another, where one of their number is injured in an accident. While they hang around waiting for his leg to be set, another gang, led by Chino (Lee Marvin), arrives. After some reasonably good-natured fisticuffs between the two leaders Chino is taken to the town jail for sassing the local policeman. So both gangs wait, drink and vroom up and down the main street. Tension rises.

Johnny, meanwhile, has become attracted to the young waitress (Mary Murphy), only to find out that she's the sheriff's daughter. The tension eventually spills over into an attempt to break out Chino and an attempted gang-rape of the waitress. Johnny averts the latter, but when she starts questioning his lifestyle he retreats into his armor of "cool."

Around about this point the movie falls apart, a fact which can be partly explained by the intervention of the censors. They considered the original screenplay downright communistic. Showing thugs creating mayhem was one thing, giving them motivation was something else altogether. They would look like heroes! One line about "the need for release from meaningless jobs" was the last straw—if that wasn't communistic then what was?

So Johnny was allowed no motivation, and the moment he's called upon to express anything other than blind rebellion the story collapses. As Brando put it: "We started out to do something worthwhile, to explain the psychology of the hipster. But somewhere along the way we went off the track. The result was that instead of finding out why young people tend to bunch into groups that seek expression in violence, all that we did was show the violence."

This was slightly ingenuous of him. They hadn't gone off the track *voluntarily,* they'd been forced off. Still, something of the original conception remained, enough to make *The Wild One* another breakthrough for both star and industry. It was, as Gavin Lambert wrote at the time, "one of the rare films in which violence is shown to have any meaning beyond a compulsive outburst of frustration or anger." For at least the first hour the level of tension was wonderfully sustained by Lazlo Benedek's direction and

Young love never runs smooth. With Mary Murphy in *The Wild One*

Brando's performance. Despite everything, as another reviewer noted, it was "never less than a serious work."

The film itself may have passed into history, obviously dated by the more violent, more socially-searching movies which it bred in the decades to follow, but the central performance by Brando still seems as fresh today as it did thirty years ago. As Rene Jordan says in his beautifully-written summation: "His first impact is devastating; as he takes possession of the town's diner the Wild One is a dangerous, barely leashed destructive force of nature. The hips are thrust forward in sexual aggression; the inner rhythm is externalized by fingers that snap to some unheard music or struggle to strike a match on a thumbnail. Every gesture is a signpost to a personal angst that cannot be verbalized. When it is, it becomes a mumble, as if the onrushing thoughts were smashing the structure of the sentences. The easy shrug, the tilted head, the roving eyes that can't look straight—all the elements are there, compressed into a ten-minute tour de force that ranks amongst the most exciting theatrical entrances ever captured on film."

This Brando, unlike Kowalski or Zapata, is a standard-bearer for youth, and his sideburns, his overt sexuality, his grooving to the jukebox, are all several years ahead of Presley. Though much of the character now seems commonplace, in 1954 it was dynamite. More important still, Johnny, unlike Kowalski, does not domesticate his conflicts—he spills them out as a challenge to the contemporary world. He is truly anti-social and truly anti-heroic. When asked what he's rebelling against he has the perfect answer, one that would reverberate through the decades to come—"whaddya got?"

THE DOCKER'S TALE

On the Waterfront, Brando's third film with Elia Kazan, is probably the best known of his early triumphs, and the character he plays in it is often perceived as the most archetypal of his early

The wild one

career. Terry Malloy is an ordinary New York docker with extraordinary connections. His brother Charley (Rod Steiger) is the right-hand man of corrupt union boss Johnny Friendly (Lee J. Cobb), who to all intents and purposes controls the local waterfront, distributing work and largesse like a feudal baron. The only real threat to his kingdom comes from outside, from politicians eager to "clean up" the waterfront. They want dockers to testify before their crime commission; Friendly, naturally enough, prefers silence.

The film begins with Terry luring a friend and potential testifier into the arms of Friendly's goons. He thinks they're only going to "lean" on the miscreant, but they hurl him off the apartment building roof to his death. This shakes Terry, and his conscience is further stirred when the dead man's sister Edie (Eva Marie Saint) damns the killers and announces her intention to see them brought to justice. She's supported by the local priest (Karl Malden), who's also decided that it's time to make a stand.

Terry falls in love with Edie, and from this point on he's torn between his loyalty to brother Charley and Friendly—"he took you to baseball when you were a kid"—and the intertwined demands of love and conscience. And of course there's also the matter of his own safety.

Eventually he agrees to testify, his mind finally made up when Charley is murdered for failing to keep him in line. After appearing before the commission he turns up for work at the docks and is refused. He then goes for Friendly, beats him in a fair fight, but can't stand against the combined force of assembled goons. The assembled crowd of dockers then refuse to work unless Terry does, and the film ends with him leading them, staggering, through the yard doors.

This ending, or rather an interpretation of it, was used by future director Lindsay Anderson as the centerpiece of a swingeing attack on the film in *Sight and Sound*. Throughout the movie, Anderson claimed, Terry is concerned only with himself, and it is only when he proves himself a stronger man than Friendly that the dockers agree, sheep-like to transfer their allegiance. No other explanation than personal charisma is given for Friendly's pre-eminent position; no social context is provided to explain the choices confronting the characters. It all added up, in Anderson's view, to a "fascist" film.

The first of his points, that Terry is concerned only with himself, is demonstrably false, but the rest of his critique has some substance. Grainy photography is no substitute for social realism, and a single shot of Friendly's invisible bosses doesn't add up to putting crime in a social context. Both Friendly and the priest are grossly overdrawn characters, more like images of dark and light than real people in a recognizable setting. And the ending, with its heavy emphasis on individual solutions to social problems—the collective response has already been routed by Friendly's goons—is, if not fascist, undeniably romantic.

A further criticism of the film, widely aired, was that Kazan had used it, had indeed made it, to justify his own position on testifying before the House Un-American Activities Committee. It's certainly hard to escape the obvious parallels; the way the choice facing Terry is presented—ratting on one's colleagues versus ratting on oneself—sounds very like Kazan stating his own defense.

But, so what? None of this criticism is really to the point. *On the Waterfront* is an American movie made in 1953 by Elia Kazan, and it inevitably bears the mark of the time and the maker. It was not intended as the sort of schematic left-wing drama which Anderson's critique implicitly demands. Ninety-nine percent of the people who saw it, even at the time, did not experience it as a defense of Kazan's political position. Nor did they know that the character upon whom Terry Malloy was based had a less fortunate time of it than the film's hero. They saw a movie about moral choices, set in a conflict environment which was recognizably typical of the times, which worked as entertainment.

It still works today. The visual mood is beautifully sustained: the trees in the foggy park seem like poetry. The dialogue is near-perfect, as are the performances of Brando, Saint and Steiger. The latter captures exactly the right blend of bravado, insecurity, brotherly concern and selfishness; Eva Maria Saint does wonders with a difficult, underwritten part, combining fragility and strength into a convincing whole. Brando is simply magnificent.

Overleaf:
Innocence amid the corruption. With Eva Marie Saint in *On the Waterfront*

At the time he considered it his finest performance to date—
"*Streetcar* was just as effective, but then I had more part under
me"—and the years have not eroded the subtleties he brought to
the part.

Two scenes are particularly memorable. The first occurs when

The mob's revenge. (*On the Waterfront*)

he's walking with Edie, wanting to express his feelings but held back by the knowledge that he's been an accessory to her brother's murder. Kazan takes up the story: "As they were walking she accidentally dropped her glove; and Brando picked up the glove; and by holding it, she couldn't get away—the glove was his way of holding her. Furthermore, whereas he couldn't, because of this tension, demonstrate any sexual or loving feeling towards her, he could towards the glove. And he put his hand inside the glove, you remember, so that the glove was both his way of holding on to her against her will, and at the same time he was able to express through the glove, something he couldn't express to her directly." This, Kazan thought, was a typical "Method" example of the use of objects, "partly accidental and partly the talent of the actor."

The second scene, perhaps the most famous few minutes of Brando's career, takes place in the back of a taxi-cab. Charley is trying to persuade Terry that he shouldn't testify, that he should stay loyal, and Terry, looking back, is thinking out loud as to what that loyalty has already cost him. He'd been a boxer once, a good one with a chance of a title-shot until he'd been ordered to throw a fight by Friendly. "I couldda been a contender" he muses wonderingly, "I couldda had class, been something more than a bum. Which is what I am." And Charley, his brother Charley, had helped to hold him back, had been disloyal to him. "It was you, Charley, it was you" he realizes. In this scene Terry comes alive as both himself and as a figment of the collective imagination. Who doesn't think that he or she could have been a contender?

Terry Malloy is an ordinary man, everyman. He's aggressive and he's vulnerable, a man and a child, torn by loyalties that cannot be reconciled. Brando's performance conveys it all, makes sense of the conflicts. If, in the end, *On the Waterfront* is one more case of "a man's gotta do what a man's gotta do," at least it's a real man, a real human being in a situation where it's far from clear what it is he's gotta do. And because the person involved is real, the fact that he does what he's gotta do becomes less important than what doing it does to him.

This time around Brando could not be denied. At the fourth time of nominating he won the Oscar, his pleasure obvious for all to see. The stage actor and the rebel had taken on Hollywood and triumphed, weaving in the process the purplest of purple patches, a string of six near-perfect performances. It had never been done before, and never since. How long could he keep it up?

"BRANDO"

There have been many great stars and many great stars and many great actors, but great actor-stars are rare, and for good reason. Great acting and stardom demand different, contradictory attributes. An actor's most priceless gift is range, a star's is an identifiable niche in the public mind, an image, a persona, to which the audience can continually relate. An actor-star is constantly engaged in a two-front war; as the actor stretches the star retracts.

As an actor Brando, according to the director who knew him best, had "everything . . . terrific feeling and violence, he has great intelligence, he's extremely intuitive. He is bisexual in the way an artist should be: he sees things both as a man and as a woman. He's strong in his sympathies to people, to all small people on the set. He's a very honest man in that he speaks plainly to you. He's also a very devious man, in that he conceals his processes and reactions; they're none of your business. He even surprises the other actors. Sometimes you don't even know that he's acting: he does something and you say: "Oh yes, he is! He's doing it!" He's very, very underground—you don't know *how* he gets to what he gets."

He obviously applied his intelligence to the business of acting. He soon learnt, as Maximilian Schell noted, that "in these times an actor cannot say 'I love you' but has to cover his feelings with a gesture." He learnt that realism demanded a certain level of inarticulacy, because most people are usually inarticulate. He learnt that the hands, the eyes, the body could speak as loud as words—the notion of "body language" could have been invented by him.

He thought about his roles, thought himself into them as

Beaten, bloodied, but decidedly unbowed. Karl Malden checks Brando's teeth in *On the Waterfront*

"Method" dictated, thought them into himself. Kazan found that he constantly came up with "ideas that were better than the ones I had. All he'd do was nod. I'd tell what I wanted, he'd nod, and then

he'd go out and do it better than I could have hoped it would be."
In Kazan's opinion, if the role was within Brando's range "which
is large, nobody can compare with him."

He's already proved how "large" it was. With six films behind
him Brando had portrayed intelligence (Antony) and slowness
(Malloy), the patrician (Antony) and the peasant (Zapata), the
meek (Malloy) and the overbearing (Kowalski), the wildness of
youth (Johnny) and the agonies of responsibility (Zapata), the
exuberance of physicality (Kowalski) and the tragedy of
immovability (Wilozek). There seemed no limit to what he might
achieve as an actor pure and simple; already there was enough on
film to justify Kazan's later assertion that Brando was "the only
genius I've ever met in the field of acting."

But Brando himself was more than a blank sheet on which he
wrote his roles; the multi-faceted actor reflected a multi-faceted
personality. Stella Adler thought she had "taught him nothing. I
opened up possibilities of feeling, thinking, experiencing, and as I
opened these doors he walked straight through." He was opening
up himself; as Eva Marie Saint said after working with him on
Waterfront, "he was like an open wound." It was this self-opening
which made him a star. Because on screen he was opening up more
than himself or a single character—he was laying bare an age.

Essentially, he expressed two conflicting realities, the man
inside the animal and the animal inside the man. The former was
the poet, the gentle rejoinder to a world of men who ought to know
better, to the idea of the man which society approved, competitive,
domineering, motivated by the desire for self-aggrandizement and
the fear of being alone. The latter was the sexual being, the ruthless
innocent, who lived in a world where feelings were repressed,
where physicality was a matter for shame. Terry Malloy was the
man inside the animal, Kowalski the animal inside the man. The
one a brutalized angel, the other an angelic brute.

These were two sides of the same coin, and the coin itself was a
whole man, a real human being. There was no age limit to this
being: his alienation was not simply the alienation of youth,
though, as *The Wild One* showed, that was part of its potential.
Ultimately the persona reflected alienation from a society which

precluded self-expression, and that society could comprise small town "squares," corrupt unions, the Mexican landed aristocracy, even a stuck-up sister-in-law.

There was, perhaps, a class limit. The character had to be capable of at least partial redemption; the tendrils of corruption must not have taken root in his soul. Powerlessness was an important attribute; he had to be hidebound by the needs of survival if salvation was to be won purely by the self-discovery of his own humanity. Temporary escape could only be found in the partial realization of his "poetry"—Zapata's horse, Johnny's bike, Terry's pigeons.

The character would inevitably suffer. Living in a corrupt world he was doomed to confusion, to divided loyalties. He would even be responsible, in two films, for his brother's death. He would try to hide his confusion in a variety of ways—the more he felt, the more necessary his shield of "cool," the clearer his feelings, the more tumbled the words. The poet would be inarticulate, the animal overly physical as if to compensate for all that held him back. At every stage others would attempt either to drag him back to their level or to channel the power of his innocence towards their own ends. And when, despite all their efforts, he chose "wholeness," humanity, he would be beaten, ridiculed, nailed to a cross. He would suffer for us, the audience, and so bring hope. He would show us that Zapatas could turn their back on corruption, that Malloys could take on the mighty, that the human spark could still shine amidst the bullshit.

This, for twenty years, was Brando the star. "Brando." The innocent underdog clawing his way up towards the light, the cinema's incarnation of redemption, the animal and the poet hidden deep within our civilized man.

PART 2
HOLLYWOOD'S REVENGE

TINSELITIS

Six good Hollywood movies in a row stretched the bounds of credibility. If he kept it up the industry would likely succumb to an epidemic of blown minds. But, fortunately for the potential sufferers, Brando now committed himself to a project which epitomized all that he had previously decried; *The Egyptian* was what Hollywood called a costume drama, and what everyone else called a succession of dramatic costumes.

He'd agreed to do it because his father advised that more money was needed quickly for the Nebraska cattle ranch into which his earnings were being channeled. Probably he comforted himself with the thought that the part would extend his range as an actor, and might be fun. If so, the first reading of the script offered instant disillusionment. According to Carlo Fiore, Brando told him "the whole thing was so bad, so Hollywood bad, that I just couldn't do it. I told Zanuck (the producer) that, and you wouldn't believe what he said. He said, "Look at it this way Marlon. You're in the trenches, see? And you've got to go over the top. You don't want to go over the top, but you've *got to*, see?" Imagine! I went back to my hotel and packed."

Which didn't please Zanuck or his company, Twentieth Century-Fox, which slapped a two million-dollar suit against the actor for breach of contract. So much for quick money. The only way Brando could get out of the suit was to sign for another costume drama, this time one set in Napoleonic France. At least he would get to play the French demi-god, and cinema actors have always considered that role as something of a challenge.

Given the right film, that is. *Desirée*, unfortunately, was not particularly interested in Napoleon, history, emotional reality, or anything that might detract from the costumes. Adapted from a bestseller—in this context the words sound like a knell of doom—the film manages to explain twenty crucial years of European history in terms of one unrequited relationship. It's as if Barbara Cartland had re-written *Das Kapital*. We learn that it was Desirée (Jean Simmons) who loaned Napoleon his fare to Paris, little

Previous page:
Brando and Jean Simmons seek mutual solace in *Desirée*

Napoleon on the telephone

realizing that once ensconced in the capital the ungrateful wretch would fall for Josephine (Merle Oberon). Not to worry though: Desirée is soon being consoled by dashing Marshal-to-be Bernadotte (Michael Rennie). Meanwhile Napoleon conquers Europe, has himself crowned, drops Josephine for Marie-Louise and makes the odd pass at the now-married Desirée. She goes to Sweden with Bernadotte, but finds it cold. Napoleon gnashes his teeth and invades Russia, etc. etc. Eventually he is persuaded to surrender, not, as previously assumed, by his military realism, but by Desirée's charming entreaties. The End.

The direction is as innovative as the script. Gowns swish on marble stairways, poses are struck, de-struck and re-struck, more gowns swish on marble stairways. The men act like men should, the women act like men think they should, and the whole thing is awful. Brando contrives odd moments of powerful acting which seem completely out of place. He later said: "I wasn't going to break my neck playing Napoleon in that picture. I got as many laughs out of the part as I could, and that was it. I went to see it, expecting to be amused. But I was only depressed. It was my own fault. If I'd had any sense, I would have handled the situation better." More pithily, he called *Desirée* "a serious retrogression and the most shaming experience of my life."

Guys and Dolls didn't set the arts on fire either. Again, the size of his fee—$200,000—seems to have offered the prime motivation, and again the point was made that the role on offer would extend his range. "I've always played lugubrious, heavy things and neglected this side of the entertainment business," he said. "Song and dance is part of an actor's trade; he should be able to dance a jig or tell a joke as part of his bag of tricks. It's just as important as telling a story poignantly and beautifully, with some kind of grace and power." Judging from his choice of words he was trying to convince himself as much as anyone else.

Still, as musicals go, *Guys and Dolls* seemed a reasonable proposition. The story was so-so, the songs mostly excellent, and it had already been a smash hit on Broadway. The major studios had fought hard for the rights, bidding each other up to $800,000 before Sam Goldwyn took the prize. He wanted Gene Kelly for

Brando and Simmons in the only good scene from *Guys and Dolls*

the role of Sky Masterson, but a piqued MGM refused to release him. Brando was the second choice.

His co-stars were Frank Sinatra and, again, Jean Simmons. Relations between the two men started out icy and grew colder. Sinatra was allegedly still sulking over his failure to land the part of Terry Malloy in *Waterfront,* and here he was playing second romantic fiddle to the man who had won an Oscar for it. On top of that he liked to shoot scenes with a minimum number of takes, whereas Brando liked to work his way into them, peaking somewhere about Take 30. Filming had hardly started before the set seemed like an armed camp, with Sinatra and entourage on one side and the rest of the cast on the other. Brando, for his part, was incensed by Sinatra's refusal to act his role as written; the singer was creating a second romantic lead and unbalancing the story. When Brando asked director Mankiewicz to do something about it, the latter simply shrugged his impotence. Brando's residual faith in directors, perhaps over-inflated by his association with Kazan, was beginning to drain away.

The film turned out to be turgid. It is far too long, lacks the spontaneity of a stage version, yet still looks too stagey. Brando's singing is passable without being notable, and the only scene with any real spark of life is that between him and Simmons in the Havana nightclub. Sky Masterson, as a character, is about as believable as the plot of *Desirée.* As Brando admitted several years later, in *Guys and Dolls* he'd "run aground."

Commercially though, the two films probably exceeded his expectations. Both were huge successes—even *Desirée* outgrossed *On the Waterfront*—and the actor had proved that his range was wider than many had feared. But there was still a sense that Brando was losing his way. Star-appeal, in his case, was inextricably bound up with "rebel-appeal," and both were bound up with his own attitudes towards his work and his life. Reading the interviews he gave around this time it is striking how out-of-character they sound: there is little of that rebellious assurance which marked earlier and later expressions of opinion.

His personal life was hardly going smoothly. His mother had died early in 1954, leaving a void in his life which couldn't be filled.

His relationships with women seemed to offer no lasting contentment. To friends, he seemed increasingly unreachable. And yet his public face had never been more "reasonable." He regretted, he told Bob Thomas, the way "I allowed myself to be handled publicity-wise when I started in pictures. It made me look like an asshole. But you don't get a second chance, and they came out of the cave and gave me the business. I was the hot-copy boy who scratched his ass and pissed on the rug."

He was less scathing about Hollywood. European movies were better, but Americans had not been "concerned with subtleties. We've been too busy building a continent. But I think we'll catch up in the end." The tone throughout was conciliatory. "If you live in society, you have to make concessions. You can't fight these things or people will beat you to death. And I can understand it. When you challenge their stand, you strike at the very heart of their existence."

Compromise seemed to be the order of the day.

INTERNATIONALIZATION

The goal was still the same. "They say in Hollywood that if you want messages, to go to Western Union," he observed. "People are not interested in the message picture, but entertainment." But he still believed that "a combination of both is possible and essential, particularly in the international exchange of ideas." His next three films would set out to show that this was so; all would be concerned with inter-cultural, inter-racial situations, all would present Americans with a different view of themselves, as seen from outside. All would offer a message draped in entertainment.

The Teahouse of the August Moon started life as a Broadway hit. Brando saw it four times and thought it "simply great—I laughed so hard I almost ended up beating the lady's hat in front of me." The story unfolds on the Japanese islands of Okinawa, where the newly arrived American victors are supervising a rehabilitation program. The dumb Captain Fisby is in charge, but soon the villagers, led by the wily interpreter Sakini, are seducing him into their Oriental lifestyle, and irrelevances like school construction give way to essentials like teahouse construction. The Americans also build a still, but this idyllic new era is abruptly shattered by the unexpected arrival of shocked superiors, who order the teahouse destroyed. Fortunately these superiors also have superiors, and the latter decide that the village is an example of local initiative worth encouraging. The teahouse is saved, and everything ends happily. En route a number of points have been made about the need for inter-cultural understanding. Hence Brando's view that the story was as socially significant as it was funny.

He was initially offered the Fisby role, but chose instead the Japanese Sakini. He looks right and he doesn't look like Brando. His accent was said by experts to be correct for an Okinawan dialect Japanese-speaker. No wonder *Sight and Sound* thought the performance "beautifully worked out," revealing "a deeply conscientious artist."

But more than Brando was needed to save this film. In the stage version Sakini had played a raconteur's role, popping up every now and then to "explain" what was happening, but in the film version most of this was left out. After introducing the story with a witty prologue—

> In Okinawa, no locks on doors. Bad manners not to trust neighbors. In America, lock and key big business. Conclusion—bad manners good business. In Okinawa, wash self in public bath with nude lady quite proper. Picture of nude lady in private home quite improper. In America, statue of nude lady in park win prize; but nude lady in flesh in park win penalty. Conclusion—pornography matter of geography.

—Sakini disappears for long stretches and the film's hold disappears with him. Glenn Ford is competent as Fisby, but basically it's just one more of those bumbling comedies with the one central joke—in this case, the naivety of Americans abroad—being milked to exhaustion and beyond.

The wily oriental. As Sakini in *The Teahouse of the August Moon*

Overleaf: A meeting of cultures, sort of. With Glenn Ford and Machiko Kyo in *The Teahouse of the August Moon*

The next film, *Sayonara*, lacked even laughs. James Michener had written the bestseller, and friend and director Joshua Logan had acquired the screen rights. Logan had almost directed *Streetcar*, and he'd tried to get Brando for *Mr. Roberts*, so it was no surprise when he contacted the actor again. This time the actor was enthusiastic. He wanted to work with Logan, whose reputation then was higher than it is now, he liked the idea of going back to Japan, which had fascinated him. Warners were offering a large fee, plus a percentage, plus generous expenses. And the story seemed to have some social point: it revolved around institutional racism in the U.S. Army, with particular reference to the practice of forbidding mixed marriages between soldiers of the occupation forces and their Japanese hosts.

Brando's enthusiasm apparently abated when he saw the script, but by then he was committed. Once on the set, he also lost faith in Joshua Logan. The director seemed more concerned with making a travelogue than a serious movie about racial intolerance, and there's a strong suspicion that his respect for Brando-the-actor was interpreted by the latter as weakness.

As in *Teahouse*, Brando had opted for the unlikely role. Joe Kelly, like Fisby in the previous film, was the obvious choice, but the actor thought "anyone" could play Kelly. "It's all written out." The Southerner, Major Gruver, on the other hand, was a real challenge. It would be "interesting to play someone who was pompous and superior and square." He remembered the type from Shattuck days.

Sayonara is set in the recent past, in the years of the Korean War. Gruver, suffering from combat fatigue, is given an easy job in Japan thanks to the influence of his prospective father-in-law, General Webster. His fiancée arrives to see him, but their already shaky grip on a mutual future soon becomes dogged by—one is tempted to say the script—the issue of Japanese-American relations. That is to say, relationships. Gruver's friend Bailey is criticized by the general's wife for bringing a Japanese girlfriend through the sacred portals of the officers' club, his fiancée is visibly moved by the attractions of a Japanese dancer, and Gruver himself agrees to act as best man at the wedding of another friend,

Kelly, to his Japanese sweetheart. Perhaps feeling left out, Gruver finds yet another Japanese girl to fall in love with. The powers-that-be view this plague of inter-racial romance with all the compassion one expects from powers-that-be, and decide to ship the mixed marriage men home, minus their new wives. Kelly and his pregnant bride commit suicide, and the rules are changed in time for Gruver and his new fiancée to defy convention and marry.

Sayonara lasts two and a half hours, and it feels more like days. The director seems more interested in endless romantic walks through beautiful Japanese gardens than making points, though it must be noted that in making the film he was forced to seek the cooperation of the very powers that the story took to task. Brando's insistence on reversing the end of the novel was also a mistake. His intentions were honorable enough—he thought that a final tragic parting would weaken the film's affirmation of mixed marriage. But Hollywood movies don't work that way; if the ending's happy the audience can quite happily forget all the implied criticism which has preceded it. If the problem is solved in terms of the leading characters, then it's solved, period.

Brando seemed relatively satisfied. He admitted that there were lots of "hearts and flowers and soft violins," but still thought the film attacked "prejudices that exist on the part of the Japanese as well as ourselves." The critics were not so impressed, though most admired Brando's own performance. The public flocked to see the film, but whether they shared the actor's reasons for liking it seems rather doubtful.

The third of the three films with an internationalist flavor was the best. Irwin Shaw's *The Young Lions* was a good book as bestsellers go, a vividly drawn story of three men, two American and one German, caught up in World War Two. They only meet at the end, in the moment of the German's death, and the book's two-sided view of the war was, structurally at least, innovative. The major weakness was the one-dimensionality of the German, and it was this that Brando, signed to play him in the film, was determined to set right. Twentieth Century-Fox, moreover, wanted him badly enough to swallow any misgivings they had

Major Gruver in
Sayonara

about conceding control over the German portion of the script.

The character of Christian Diestl was adjusted accordingly. Brando said that the film would "try to show that Nazism is a matter of mind, not geography, that there are Nazis—and people of good will—in every country. The world can't spend its life looking over its shoulder and nursing hatreds. There would be no progress that way." He told Shaw, who disagreed but had no direct

Interracial goings-on. With Miiko Taka in *Sayonara*

Go on, have two!
With May Britt
in *The Young
Lions*

influence over the film's making, that "if we continue to say that all Germans are bad, we add to the Nazi's argument that all Jews are bad."

The new Diestl was brought to a sense of shame by the war, not brutalized by it as he had been in the novel. Brando handled the transition superbly, turning in one of his best performances, understated and eerily real. There are echoes of his earlier films here, not surprisingly perhaps, since this model of a man slowly awakening to a sense of social-moral responsibility was a unifying factor in those earlier films.

And, if on a rather more mundane level, the film as a whole also worked well. Director Edward Dymtryk kept it moving, yet managed to leave enough space between the excitingly-staged action sequences for the odd glimmer of reflection. Montgomery Clift and Dean Martin were both more than adequate. *The Young Lions* turned out as involving as the best Hollywood product of that era could be.

But was it the film that Brando envisaged? He'd got across the point that Germans are human too, but there wasn't much sign of Nazis in the Allied camp. A little anti-semitism perhaps, but that's soon sorted out. The film's thrust was clearly anti-war on a philosophical plane, but most of the philosophy seemed to be coming out of the barrel of a gun. *The Young Lions* had not escaped its origins; it was still essentially a Hollywood product, made with commercial considerations uppermost in mind and bearing the mark of all the necessary compromises.

Things didn't have to be that way. The same year saw the release of *Paths of Glory,* Stanley Kubrick's second feature film. Comparing the two, Brando (who saw Kubrick's when considering him for the direction of *One-Eyed Jacks*) cannot but have been struck by the difference. One was entertainment with a few things to say, the other, for all its lack of spectacular effects, was just as entertaining, just as gripping, yet still managed to pack the sort of philosophical punch which Brando was looking for.

And which, in three films, he'd failed to find. All had been commercial successes, but perhaps he now took that for granted. They had also extended his range as an actor, if at the cost of

Diestl reaches the end of his tether in *The Young Lions*

Overleaf: Director for the only time; Brando takes to the skies on the set of *One-Eyed Jacks*

blurring his image. But it's hard to believe that they had significantly advanced "the international exchange of ideas."

LOOKING FOR A WESTERN

Like most stars—like most people, come to that—Brando tended to blame the self-defined shortcomings of his work on the limitations imposed by others. These "others" were both general—the studio system, the state of Hollywood consciousness —and particular. How, for example, could he make a coherent statement about racism if Joshua Logan insisted on shooting a travelogue around him? How could he make his point with Diestl if Montgomery Clift vetoed his death in a crucified pose? He had to have more control over his career. He had to have the final say.

Early in 1956, before leaving for Japan and *Sayonara*, he had set up his own movie company as the vehicle for realizing such control. His partners in Pennebaker—named after his mother— were his father and George Englund, a friend and up-and-coming producer-director. The prospects looked bright. The studios were losing their long battle with TV, and the bigger stars could not demand and get most of what they wanted from the besieged industry. Brando was still one of the biggest.

Two projects were announced almost immediately. One was to be based on the work of the UN technical assistance program in East Asia. It would center around the disappearance of a UN research worker in Indo-China, would be an adventure story full of political content. Englund was to direct from a script by Stewart Stern, and Brando, who had just completed a "stimulating" 20,000 mile tour of the area in question, would both oversee the production and star in the movie.

This project was scrapped for reasons that remain obscure, leaving attention focused on the other, a western. This would eventually be brought to fruition, but only after a long succession of metamorphoses. The original idea of cinematizing a bestseller, *To Tame A Land*, was soon abandoned due to script problems.

Brando then decided to write his own western, and over the next year or so spent much of his spare time creating *A Touch of Vermilion*. Eventually a 240-page script was submitted to Paramount, who rejected it.

Why a western? Well, it's hard to believe in the eighties, but way back in the fifties the western was one of, if not *the* pre-eminent genre in American film-making. They were popular with audiences, and for this if no other reason, were considered important by Hollywood. Many were being made in the studios, and TV was getting in on the act with its own series. If Brando made a western, he was certain of a ready-made audience.

More to the point perhaps, the usual western was full of the clichéd approach which Brando hated. Quality westerns were certainly being made, but in most cases it was very much a matter of known quality—innovative westerns were in short supply. Movies like *The Man from Laramie, 3.10 to Yuma, Rio Bravo, Warlock* and *The Magnificent Seven,* all made in the latter half of the fifties, were as conventional as they were excellent. *The Sheepman* and *Run of the Arrow* had something to say, and *The Left-Handed Gun* served notice of Arthur Penn's illustrious future, but the only western of this period to show any real socio-psychological depth was John Ford's extraordinary and untypical *The Searchers*.

So a western offered Brando the best of both worlds, a chance to stretch the bounds of convention in front of an assured mass audience. If only he could find the right story.

Pennebaker meanwhile was going nowhere fast. The company had shared in the production of *Sayonara* and *The Young Lions,* but with no new Brando projects of their own, Englund's successors Glass and Seltzer began producing non-Brando movies: *Shake Hands with the Devil, Paris Blues* and *The Naked Edge*. These kept the ledgers ticking and the hands busy, but in no way contributed towards a fulfilling of the company's original purpose.

At last the right script—or the beginnings of a basis for a script—turned up. Producer Frank P. Rosenberg had bought the film rights to Charles Neider's *The Authentic Death of Hendry Jones,* and his scriptwriter on another project, Sam Peckinpah, had

Rio and the Mona Lisa, *One-Eyed Jacks*

Overleaf: Dad Longworth assuages his guilt. With Karl Malden in *One-Eyed Jacks*

asked if he could attempt the screenplay. Rosenberg had agreed with some reluctance, but thought well enough of the finished product to submit it to MCA. They passed it on to Brando—few people in California can have been unaware that the actor was looking for a western script—and he liked it. As a basis. Rosenberg was brought in to produce as part of the deal.

Who would direct? This was a problem, and perhaps one not fully appreciated by Brando. He wanted a good director—who would want a bad one?—but he'd set up Pennebaker and this film as means for furthering his own control over his output. There was bound to be a conflict of interests here, for what good director would submit to taking orders from an actor, no matter how eminent the latter might be?

Brando decided on Kubrick after seeing his first two films—*The Killing* and *Paths of Glory*—at the suggestion of a friend. Kubrick wanted the script completely re-written, and called in Calder Willingham to assist him in the task. Months of interminable script conferences followed, with the major participants unable to find a common vision of the finished product. Brando was fairly clear as to what he wanted: "I have the obligation and the opportunity . . . to try to communicate the things I think are important . . . to make a frontal attack on the temple of clichés." He wanted to "scramble" good and evil in the characters, to make them real. Kubrick's views are not known, but some deductions can be made from his later work. Over the years he was to mount his own assault on the temple, but not through the development of realistic characters; he tended to work more on European lines, seeing characters as elements of the overall imagery. It seems reasonable to suppose that his wish to replace the already-signed Karl Malden with Spencer Tracy was formed with such an approach in mind; Malden was a good enough actor but Tracy had the stronger image.

Brando refused to break his promise to Malden, and eventually lost patience with Kubrick. The director was either fired or chose to quit—versions differ. A replacement was needed quickly, and Brando suggested himself after sounding out several experienced alternatives. Paramount agreed; how else was the film going to get made? Brando had a free hand at last, and one suspects that he greeted the prospect with both apprehension and elation. The assault on the "temple of clichés" would be his to lead and his to answer for should it fail.

ONE-EYED MOVIE

At this stage of the process, with shooting about to begin, the newly-titled *One-Eyed Jacks* represented an amalgam of the traditional and the innovative. The hero-figure was clearly in the latter mold. According to Brando: "Our early day heroes were not brave one hundred per cent of the time nor were they good one hundred per cent of the time." The character of Rio would reflect this reality. He would be "intuitive and suspicious, proud and searching," with "a touch of the vain and a childish and disproportionate sense of virtue and manly ethics." Like this principal adversary Dad Longworth (Karl Malden), Rio would be a "one-eyed jack" in both intended senses, a "wild card" and a man who shows only one side of his character to the world. His relationship with the traditional female interest would be characterized by a similar ambivalence.

The basic plot structure was more conventional: a man who thinks himself betrayed seeks, and eventually finds, revenge in the time-honored manner. In the process he finds himself loved by the female interest. The settings were a mixture of the familiar and the novel, with the story moving through Ford's desert, into Hawks' town, and down to Brando's Pacific beaches. This last feature might not seem so revolutionary now, but back in 1961 the sight of Rio practicing his draw against the backdrop of crashing surf seemed startlingly original.

As a director Brando turned out to be the ultimate in perfectionists. Before shooting began in December 1958 he painstakingly oversaw the costuming, casting, set design and locations. He didn't believe in using extras on the usual rent-a-crowd lines; everyone on the set was expected to *act*, no matter how small the part. Those gathered to watch Longworth whipping Rio were encouraged, "Method"-style, to think their own terrible thoughts, and to aid their concentration a bonus was offered for the most horrified expression. He was extremely patient in bringing a performance out of his inexperienced leading lady, Pina Pellicer. In fact, he was extremely patient with everyone, everything. According to producer Rosenberg, Brando "pondered each camera set-up while 120 members of the company sprawled on the ground like battle-weary troops . . . every line every actor read, as well as every button on every piece of wardrobe got Brando's concentrated attention until he was completely satisfied."

The consequences of this devotion to detail were becoming apparent as early as the evening of the first day's shooting. They'd succeeded in shooting one-sixth of the scheduled script pages and were thus, as one producer wittily observed, already five days behind schedule. The two months of shooting originally envisaged became six months, with Brando breaking the unofficial world record for the amount of film exposed in pursuit of a single movie. The budget, of course, soared with each new take, up from the allocated $1.8 million to something in the region of $6 million. It was a lot to spend on a western then.

Whether it was worth it or not the public would never know. Brando's rough cut of the film ran for six hours, and he refused to take it below four hours and forty-two minutes. Twenty years later he would call the cutting-room "one of the most awful places in the world . . . you sit all day long in a dark place filled with cigarette smoke."

Still, it's a pity he didn't see it through. The Paramount professionals took over, bringing the movie down to two hours and twenty minutes by ruthlessly excising everything but the bare essentials. Or what they considered the bare essentials. One key scene in which Rio rapes a Chinese girl while recuperating from his wounds was taken out completely, and in general it seems as if the retention of character complexity was not uppermost in the cutters' minds. To make matters even worse Paramount insisted on an upbeat ending: Rio and Louisa would not now be killed, they

Right and overleaf: Lovers. With Pina Pellicer in *One-Eyed Jacks*

would merely part with vague assurances from him that he will return.

Brando was at first furious, then stoical to the point of self-denial. *One-Eyed Jacks,* he now decided, was no more than "a potboiler." Far from being the promised assault on the temple of clichés, it was "quite conventional. It's not an artistic success. I'm a businessman. I'm a captain of industry—nothing less than that. Any pretension I've sometimes had of being artistic is now just a long, chilly hope. *One-Eyed Jacks* is a product just like—a news item. News makes money, not art. Movies are not art."

He was being much too hard on himself and the film. Even after its alleged mauling at Paramount's hands it remains one of the best westerns ever made. On traditional terms it scores highly, with Brando, Malden and Pellicer all sustaining characters that are considerably less stereotyped than those inhabiting most sagas of the sagebrush. The choreography of the violent set-pieces is uniformly excellent, and the concluding duel between Longworth and Rio is one of the most stunning ever put on film.

Rio is perhaps not the figure Brando intended, but neither is he the one-dimensional Hollywood hero. He's a thoroughly convincing liar, he treats the heroine shabbily and, most important of all, his character is not defined by idealism. There's no pretense that he's a civilizing influence, that the West will be a safer or more humane place for his presence. He's not in the least sympathetic, but he is empathetic. We see the conflicts within him, feel his hurt, understand his childish clinging to the western code of chivalry. He may not be right, but he's real.

The critics seem mostly to have missed the point. Herbert Feinstein complained that "many of the lines of the script sound like the speech of self-conscious adolescents," a strange comment to make about a film largely concerned with the problems of a self-conscious adolescent. Penelope Houston thought that Brando liked "striking attitudes" too much, that "the drive and authority of the film at its best are continually being compromised by the overbearing extravagance of the film at its worst . . . repeated images of melancholy and violence, so many cloaked figures, lone riders, sad silhouettes, take on the luxuriance of grand opera without the operatic justification."

What could the "justification" be? Like any western *One-Eyed Jacks* was more concerned with the time of its making than the time in which it was purportedly set, and in many ways it can be seen as the first "sixties western." Indeed, with its uneasy blending of gritty realism—the interiors, the squalid bars, look forward to Leone, not back to Hawks and Mann—and revolutionary romanticism it could be seen as the archetypal "sixties western." Youth clashes with hypocritcal authority, sex and love share an uneasy co-existence. They'd be selling postcards of Rio's hanging while the mermaids played in the Pacific surf. He is a sixties character, at home in both the light and the dark; the complexity of his emotional responses reflects both the squalid mix of human emotions and the beautiful/ugly world they inhabit. Like Johnny in *The Wild One* we know where he comes from.

All of which makes *One-Eyed Jacks* infinitely more than a "potboiler." The sad thing is that Brando seems really to have believed that was all he had made. His "pretensions" of "being artistic," though disavowed, would not fade away, but a real sense of disillusionment with the cinema's potential seems to have taken place. He has not directed again, and as an actor he would henceforth embrace projects with enormous ambivalence, on the one hand pooh-poohing "artistic pretensions," on the other seeking to extend each film from within, often against the director's wishes. The only good thing to come out of the whole *One-Eyed Jacks* experience was the film itself.

THE END OF INNOCENCE

The new decade had started inauspiciously for Brando in more ways than one: career, business interests, relationships, all were something of a mess. Career-wise he remained one of the top stars, but such success was no longer enough—if it ever had been—to provide him with job or any other form of satisfaction. "People have nothing in the lexicon of their own experience to know what fabulous success is," he said around this time. "They don't know the emptiness of it . . . I'm successful. I'm the Horatio Alger story. I'm the kid from the middle income bracket who never finished high school, who went the route of individualism, and made it. I've done what my country told me to do. "Go on, kid! You can do it! That's what we want you to do!" It's a fraud and a gyp. It's the biggest disappointment."

No lasting compensation was to be found in monogamy. He married Anna Kashfi in 1957, but scarcely had their son Christian been conceived than the relationship turned sour, and the ensuing battles for custody of the child would last throughout the sixties. He married Movita, whom he had known since *Zapata* days, in 1960, with whom he had a child shortly thereafter. Other relationships with France Nuyen and Rita Moreno provided hot copy for the gossip columnists.

Financially, he suddenly found himself in a disaster area. All the money he had poured into the Nebraska cattle ranch disappeared overnight, leaving him forced, for the first time in his career, to seek work for financial reasons alone. It was not just a matter of feeding himself; he now had two ex-wives, two children and the people at Pennebaker to support.

He went into *The Fugitive Kind* with a clear objective: "I needed money in a hurry. And it was the best role I could find in a hurry." This was probably true, but it didn't say much for the other roles on offer. Based on a rather lack-luster Tennessee Williams play, *Orpheus Descending,* which had done only moderate business on Broadway, *The Fugitive Kind* was not what his career needed. It was a re-tracing of old ground, and an unsatisfactory one at that. Brando didn't get on with co-star Anna Magnani, and only the scene of Val Xavier's Kafkaesque interrogation, right at the beginning of the film, showed him at his best. The other 115 minutes seemed almost parodic, with the characters swapping knowing, philosophical quips about the state of love, the Deep South and everything. There are three types of people in the world, Brando's character wryly observes, "the buyers, the bought, and those who don't belong no place at all." One guess as to which he thinks he is.

The Fugitive Kind made no sort of splash, and Brando must have wished in retrospect that his next project could have shared such anonymity. *Mutiny on the Bounty,* however, was to be one of those rare movies which attract more publicity in their making than in their showing, and Brando, with little justice, was to be made the principal villain of the piece.

The film had a typical Hollywood genesis circa 1960. Outdoing TV was the name of the current game, and large-screen epics were thought to be one of the most potent weapons in Hollywood's armory. MGM, having just done very well with a re-make of *Ben Hur,* picked the old Gable-Laughton *Bounty* as a second suitable case for re-treatment. Since they already owned the rights, the company could afford to lash out on stars and locations. A good story, the biggest names, wide-screen beauty—what could do wrong?

Aaron Rosenberg was appointed producer, but not for the best of reasons: he had had been upset at MGM for reneging on their commitment to let him produce *How the West Was Won,* and the company, then, offered him *Bounty* instead. Rosenberg's friend, John Sturges, then suggested Brando for one of the two lead roles. He initially declined, but after some consideration and a re-reading of the original Nordhoff/Hall novel trilogy, became more interested in the project. "The theme of the story intrigued me," he said. "Here was a group of men who had one great moment of glory, when they rose up and conquered tyranny. They held the greatest opportunity to achieve happiness. They went to a place where the natives were friendly, where living was incredibly easy. And what happened? Within two years they were dead. They killed each other. It seemed to me that this presented a microcosm of man's situation throughout history: the struggle of black versus white, of good versus evil, of the urge to create and the urge to destroy. If man cannot find happiness on an island paradise, where can he find it?"

If this intriguing aftermath was given due prominence in the new film version then he was vaguely interested. He met with

The mutiny begins. With Trevor Howard and Richard Harris in *Mutiny on the Bounty*

Overleaf: She wants a hat like that too! With future wife Tarita on the set of *Mutiny on the Bounty*

Rosenberg and MGM production boss Sol Siegel, but there was no apparent meeting of minds, and Brando's interest waned. Rosenberg decided to look elsewhere, and in the meantime hired the novelist Eric Ambler to fashion a screenplay.

As a "long shot" this script was sent to Brando, who didn't think it fulfilled his criteria. MGM then offered him *Lawrence of Arabia*, which he liked even less. He was still willing to do *Bounty*, he told them, if a lengthy sequence was added to a re-written script telling the story of the post-Mutiny period on Pitcairn Island. MGM bit the bullet and agreed, writing it into Brando's contract that he had script approval rights over this final section. An October 1961 starting-date was fixed. The budget would be $10 million, of which Brando would receive $500,000 down, ten per cent of the gross receipts *and* $5,000 per day for each day beyond the allotted timespan. There was still no agreed script.

Brando flew to London, partly to meet the assigned director Sir Carol Reed, but the two men spent most of their time discussing another movie the actor had in mind, one centered on the fate of the executed rapist Caryl Chessman. Meanwhile Ambler was finishing his script re-write. Brando rejected it, and two more writers—Borden Chase and William Driskill—were brought in to re-write the re-write. They couldn't satisfy everyone either: the last section could not be made to dovetail with what preceded it; anything seemed like an anti-climax after the high-point of the mutiny itself. And time had run out.

Cast and crew arrived before the custom-built *Bounty*, thanks to two fires on board during the voyage from Nova Scotia. For the first two months all attention had to be focused on the scenes set ashore, insofar as anyone could agree as to how they should go. Reed didn't like the way Bligh had been humanized in the script(s), and reportedly refused to shoot any scenes involving this version of the Captain. Brando continued refusing sections of the script(s) he had already rejected. Without a Bligh, a Christian or a boat it's difficult to imagine what *could* be shot. Milestone, who eventually replaced Reed, was probably not exaggerating when he claimed that he inherited only seven minutes of completed film.

The boat eventually arrived, but with the Tahitian rainy season close on its heels. The MGM production planners had apparently not bothered to consider anything as mundane as the local climate. The whole company was forced back to Hollywood, supposedly to shoot interiors.

The script problem, which necessarily encompassed the "character problem"—who were this Bligh and this Christian?—refused to go away, despite the non-stop efforts of Charles Lederer, the latest writer engaged to reconcile the irreconcilable. Reed, still unhappy with the script's Bligh, now took exception to Brando's Christian, and receiving no support from Rosenberg tried to resign. The MGM chiefs, displaying all the financial acumen which characterized their handling of the project overall, first refused his resignation and then sacked him. Reed thereby received the hefty compensation which resigning would have denied him.

Looking for a new director the producers sounded out Brando, who refused. They then turned to the veteran Lewis Milestone, who "felt it would be quite an easy assignment because they'd been on it for months and there surely couldn't be much more to do." Some hope! It was now Milestone's turn to tussle with Brando, who was still rightly demanding the finished script he'd been promised at the outset. Given this situation, the director's dictatorial style was wholly out of place; he complained that Brando kept asking him "why" Christian was doing this or that, but with no coherent script to work from the actor had every reason to ask. And he was completely within the terms of his contract in doing so.

Milestone soon gave up the struggle. Asked by Rosenberg one day why he wasn't watching a piece of filming he replied: "What for? When the picture is finished I'll buy a ticket and see the whole bloody mess in a theater." He might be sacked for taking such an attitude, but sacking, as Reed had inadvertently proved, was more lucrative than resigning.

MGM refused to sack him, preferring to watch the film spin out of control with no one at the wheel. The British contingent—Trevor Howard, Richard Harris, Hugh Griffiths—bitterly opposed Brando's assumption of the dropped directorial reins, but had no positive suggestions of their own to make. They alternately bitched about their co-star and lived up to their own rip-roaring reputations; according to one report Griffiths' part had to be rewritten when he was asked to leave Tahiti for rip-roaring too much.

Somehow the bulk of the film got made with Lederer churning out new script. Brando and Lederer re-writing it, Brando directing and Milestone reading magazines in his chair. But still the final section, the post-mutiny developments which had initially drawn Brando to the project, could not be agreed upon. Lederer is said to have written eleven versions, and the last of these was shot, despite Brando's objections. It was never seen though; a new ending, reportedly part-scripted by Billy Wilder, was filmed in the summer of 1962 with George Seaton directing, a full year after the completion of principal filming.

This whole sorry South Sea Saga had been conducted in the full glare of the publicity spotlight, and the knives long in wait for Brando now had their chance to flash. The most notorious attack came from Bill Davidson in the *Saturday Evening Post* under the headline "The Mutiny of Marlon Brando." The actor's alleged overweight, his alleged malingering, his alleged egotism, anything that could be used to portray Brando as the spoilt child of the movie business was dredged up, spiced with back-biting quotes, and set down as evidence for the prosecution. Suddenly all the film's problems were Brando's fault. All Hollywood's problems were Brando's fault. Nobody took much notice of Rosenberg when he admitted that MGM hadn't lived up to their agreements "about the basic concept of the picture." Nobody quoted Reed saying that he had no quarrel with Brando, that he still thought him "the most exciting actor in the world today." No mention was made of the idiocy involved in sending cast and crew to a location at the worst possible time of the year. No mention was made of anything which might deflect attention away from criticism of the star.

The film itself, after all this ballyhoo, could only be anticlimactic. But despite everything it was far from bad. The melodramatic intensity of the original version, its ranging of absolute good against absolute evil, had been replaced by a thoughtfully dramatic investigation of the mutiny and its

Brando and Tarita relax on the set of *Mutiny on the Bounty*

participants. Bligh was more credible, Christian considerably more confused. He starts out as a fop, turns into Clark Gable for the mutiny itself, and then becomes a philosopher. Brando's achievement was to make this more or less believable.

But, in a sense, the quality of his performance was neither here nor there. The film did well—it *was* epic, the locations *were* beautiful, the story was good, and *everyone* knew about the problems—but it had cost its star dear. From the industry's point of view much of the mud had stuck. Brando was too expensive, they said, too unruly, incapable of working with others, incapable of keeping his promises. A great actor perhaps, but that was the least of a movie star's attributes.

And from Brando's side the mud had stuck just as thick. He had trusted MGM and they had let him down. He'd tried to make the movie mean something, tried to make it more than just another money-spinning epic, and he'd been obstructed at every step of the way.

To hell with him, they said. To hell with them, he said. It would be another ten years before Hollywood took Marlon Brando back to its hypocritical bosom.

1934-P.10

PART 3
AN AMERICAN MISCAST

CROSSROADS OF A CAREER

The attacks on Brando's professional attitude and behavior which followed the *Bounty* imbroglio marked the culmination of a campaign of several years' duration. The ball had been set rolling by writer Truman Capote in 1957. He had interviewed—some would say conned—Brando in his Japanese hotel room during the making of *Sayonara*, and then spent nearly a year preparing his piece for publication. The star certainly seems to have let his usual defenses down that night, and Capote made the most of it: Brando came out of the piece looking like an idiot. Many of those who read the edited interview were unaware how easily that can happen to anyone who is not very practiced in dealing with an interviewer skilled at evoking an interesting story.

Brando was further attacked for refusing to return to the stage, for being too intellectual, for considering his judgment superior to that of Hollywood producers. Apparently America's press wanted an idiot with integrity. The arguments used were either specious, absurd or both. But they did reflect one reality—the widespread and genuine sense of disappointment with the way the actor's career was developing. He did seem to have lost his way.

The first six films had written a brilliant chapter in American cinematic history, had struck a nerve in American society. Looking back at the image Brando projected in these films it's possible to define it as a sort of composite Presley-Dylan image, a challenge to the repressive conformism of post-war American society that was both physical and intellectual. But in the eight films that had followed, this rebellious screen persona had been dissipated, lost in the variety of roles played. In those eight movies he had played only three young Americans, and of these Sky Masterson was more of a prop than a character. Which left Val Xavier, a role in search of a decent film, and Rio, who had been cut to shreds in the Paramount editing-room. Sakini, Gruver and Christian might have stretched his talents as an actor, but they had also served to blur the image which had made his early films so breathtakingly relevant.

Previous page: David Niven, Shirley Jones and Brando on the set of *Bedtime Story*

Brando had been attempting something of a balancing act. He had looked for films with a "message," but at the same time had sought both to retain his integrity as an actor and to remain within the mainstream of Hollywood commercial cinema. In an ideal world the three might have been mutually reinforcing; in this world they simply pulled each other down. All the messages had been diluted by the films which were supposedly carrying them, and the only lasting consequence of this idealistic approach was a growing history of disputes between Brando and the other, less-politically-minded people involved in making films with him. The *Bounty* fiasco, though hardly Brando's responsibility in the way the press implied, did arise directly from the conflict which his presence provoked. It had to be either a Hollywood epic or a film with a point: it couldn't be both. Brando should have realized this from the outset, and refused to have anything to do with the project. The producers should have realized this from the outset, and either hired someone else or re-thought their entire approach to the film; they should certainly not have given Brando script approval over *part* of the film. Everyone should have realized that there was no way that the two different conceptions could be stitched together. Hollywood didn't work like that.

But this conflict between "message" and "Hollywood" was not the only one troubling Brando. His integrity as an actor didn't gel with the message-giver either. He wasn't prepared to go through the motions in the service of a political point; the films might be set up with such an idea in mind but then the actor re-discovered his craft. Diestl's message, for example, was undercut by Brando's humanization of him; the more he made his characters understandable the more their actions seemed excusable.

Again, Brando was trying to have it both ways, to convey the complexity of human beings in his acting, in films that were supposed to be making clear and concise attacks on particular states of mind. And, again, he was losing both ways. The messages were getting lost in the Hollywood fog, and Brando himself was getting lost in the accuracy of his characterizations. He might be still a rebel and still an actor, but he was no longer the rebel-actor; he no longer spoke directly to his audience through characters

Overleaf:
MacWhite arrives in a Hollywood-style Asia – five ugly Americans, two natives and dense foliage

designed to fit him, his message.

He seems to have been aware of the problems, but the solution eluded him. He had tried to take his career by the scruff of the neck, to force the actor, the message-giver and Hollywood into a mutually-reinforcing relationship under his own direction. *One-Eyed Jacks* had been the result. He had then tried to achieve a similar end on the *Bounty* set with disastrous results. Who in Hollywood would take a risk on him now, as director or script-approving star? They would let him work, but under their terms, not his. He would be nothing more than an actor working in a director's medium and the chances of finding, in the Hollywood of 1962, a director of like mind, prepared to share the vision and the responsibility, were thin indeed. Elia Kazans didn't grow on trees.

If he couldn't pull the actor, the message-giver and Hollywood together, he would have to choose between them. He had no desire to become an actor pure and simple, to return to the stage as a sort of American Olivier. "I have no overwhelming interest in becoming a classical actor," he said, "and I do not think I would have continued in the theater. Most Broadway productions are commercially oriented. The plays are thought of in terms of a product, like toothpaste." So much for that option.

He was not the person to embrace Hollywood on its own terms, to take the "Elvis option," to rely on his natural gifts as a performer once time had blunted the cutting edge of his image. He was far too aware for that. As Paulene Kael wrote in 1966: "What crown could he aspire to? Should he be a "King" like Gable, going from one meaningless picture to another . . . Columnists don't attack that kind of king on his papier-mâché throne: critics don't prod him to return to the stage: the public doesn't turn against him." So much for that option.

The message-giver had several choices open to him. He could abandon Hollywood for the more amenable European cinema, or abandon film altogether and become a political celebrity trading on fame already won. He could split his time between acting and playing politics, pursuing each vocation in isolation from the other. But whatever he did he had to get his message straight. What, since *On the Waterfront*, had Brando been trying to say in his films?

What, in political parlance, was his current perspective?

Basically, the Brando of 1955–62 was the classic American liberal. He was concerned to correct abuses, not to overthrow the system. The poor, the minorities, the oppressed of the world, all those denied the rights and advantages which the ordinary, middle-class, white American took for granted—they were his concern, and they had been the political focus of most of his recent films. The emptiness, at some level, of those rights and advantages, the reality of white American life depicted with such devastating candor in *Streetcar, The Wild One* and *Waterfront,* no longer seemed to concern him as a film-maker. For the moment exploitation seemed a more pressing matter than alienation.

He understood the latter, of course. "There's no security in talent," he would say in 1966. "I know any number of talented people who are insecure as hell, who are riddled with a pervading sense of emptiness. Not to be a success is a sin in the U.S., but most successful people in Hollywood are failures as human beings . . . Insecurity lies all around. Marilyn Monroe's death—that stopped everyone, just for a moment. They thought: Oh God, here's a successful actress who has everything: money, beauty, adulation and a happy future—everything contained in the American Dream—and she fell. What hope is there for us?"

But his choice of projects, both before and after 1962, did not reflect this awareness. Over the next decade a profound challenge was to be mounted to America's cultural values, and insofar as individuals influence such movements, few figures in American cultural life had done more to make this challenge inevitable than Brando himself. As a person, as a political voice, he would play a role in the unfolding of events in the sixties too, but as a cinematic influence he would be almost invisible. The decade of rebellion was to be the decade of Brando's occulsion as a film star—surely one of the most striking paradoxes of the times.

It was, in fact, his veteran status as a "rebel," and the preconceptions which such a long involvement entailed, that blunted his receptivity to change. Like any classic liberal he tended to see politics as a thing apart, as an aspect of life, and it was this attitude which he carried into his films. Large sections of society,

Brando in the early sixties

1934-P50

however, were moving in the opposite direction, towards a view of politics as being no more and no less than a personal angle on life in its entirety. Everything was political. As the sixties progressed movies reflected this shift of consciousness; more and more were being made by young, up-and-coming directors which, though message-free in the old sense, were profoundly political in the new sense. They dealt, as Brando's early films had dealt, with ordinary American life, and they enabled a new breed of actor-stars to escape many of the contradictions which still plagued Brando.

A film like *Hud* (1963) might have been conceived for the actor who played Terry Malloy, Kowalski and Johnny. Its central character (played by Paul Newman) was awash with the frustrations of contemporary American society, and the film, though completely apolitical in the old sense, was clearly intended as a serious statement. It had something to say about life, and it had an impact, in the way the best movies do, on the way its audience thought about things. If Brando could have found roles and films like this, he could perhaps have held together the actor, the message-giver and his Hollywood career. But he didn't. He had too much respect for the old ways to embrace the new ideas, and too much contempt for Hollywood to abandon his old ideals. And so, for the next ten years, he would get the worst of both worlds, making films that, with a few exceptions, would lack either quality or a coherent message. His talent as an actor would always shine through, in some cases to such an extent as to unbalance the movie, but the grand plan of using routine Hollywood vehicles as celluloid soap boxes from which to address the evils of the time was doomed by its own and its author's inner contradictions.

TRAILER FOR VIETNAM

His next film, *The Ugly American,* offered a paradigm of his sixties work, with all the various "Brandos" working at cross-purposes, all with the best of intentions. The bestselling novel of the same name, written by William L. Lederer and Eugene Burdick, seemed to fill a long-standing Pennebaker requirement, a satisfactory structure for a movie about American influence in south-east Asia. Brando had been looking for something like this since his 20,000 mile tour in the mid-fifties, and after purchasing the rights, assigned fellow-tourists George Englund and Stewart Stern to direct and screenwrite respectively. The whole package, including, some say, Pennebaker itself, was then sold to Universal.

The story takes place in the fictional country of Sarkhan—i.e. Vietnam—and begins with the confirmation of Carter MacWhite (Brando) as the new American Ambassador. He knows the country from World War Two days, the notorious guerrilla leader Deong was once his friend, and his mission is to swing the country as a whole into a pro-American position.

He doesn't get off to a very good start. His car is attacked between the airport and the embassy, the latter is full of golf-happy morons, and Deong seems so anti-American that MacWhite thinks he's turned communist. He hasn't of course. Deong is a nationalist and a neutralist, and it takes MacWhite the rest of the movie to discover that such a stance is only anti-American when the Americans make it so. Deong gets killed by the communists to show that, on the contrary, his position is the best the Americans can hope for, and uses up his dying words with protestations of faith in the eventual good sense of Uncle Sam. MacWhite, suitably enlightened, returns home to spread the message that America must stop imposing its views on all and sundry. The movie's last shot is of a bored watcher turning off his TV set in the middle of a MacWhite sentence.

All of which might seem somewhat naive in the aftermath of a war which devastated the country in question, a country moreover in which there was never a real neutralist option. But the film's heart is clearly in the right place, and it does have some unusually sensible things to say. In the context of 1963 it constituted a political statement both pertinent and courageous.

As a movie, though, it's a mess. It is far too truthful, too faithful in its reporting of a complex reality, to succeed as agitprop. It's far too pessimistic and prosaic to hit the jackpot as entertainment.

Brando, as usual, was interested more in character than suspense, romance or narrative, but the more these characters are drawn out the more apparent it becomes that they're not real characters at all, merely representatives of the political attitudes which the movie-makers wanted to examine. Brando himself is just one of them; complete with mustache, suave exterior and liberal concern, MacWhite could have been played by anyone vaguely competent. So the movie loses all ways. The message is forsaken in the cause of character honesty, character honesty is forsaken in the cause of the message, and Brando the star is forsaken in the cause of both. The result: no character honesty, no clear message, no Brando.

The only thing going for *The Ugly American* was the deluge of criticism it received from the ranks of the unenlightened. Even the future Vietnam dove Senator Fulbright damned the film as anti-American, which doubtless pleased its star. "I feel that the film is critical of the U.S.," he said. "It is critical of the neutralists. And it is critical of rightist regimes who make no reforms and are not willing to make reasonable and intelligent concessions for the establishment of democracy in their countries . . . It is critical of the communists. I think there will be an enormous and perhaps bombastic reaction against this picture in some areas of America."

In some areas there was, in others it wasn't even seen. Brando's extra-curricular political activities were now beginning to affect his career, with many theaters in the South refusing to show his films because of his increasingly outspoken line on black civil rights. Several years earlier his had been one of the names appended to the famous full-page ad in the *New York Times* soliciting funds for the movement, and since then his involvement in the cause had deepened. He was one of the organizers of the spring 1963 Washington march, and later that year appeared at meetings up and down the country.

In 1964 the scope of his political activity widened further. He was the moving force behind a largely unsuccessful campaign to prevent the showing of films in segregated theaters, and he was also heavily involved in the attempt to push through guidelines for a fairer black representation in the movie industry. He became more than interested in the fate of America's native population, the

Indians, traveled throughout the West learning about Indian cultures and problems, went to Washington to plead their cause, took part in an "illegal" fish-in with Indians who had been granted the relevant river-section for "as long as the grass shall grow." He read the history books, heard the Indians' oral history, found out that he could still be shocked by the enormity of the lie perpetrated by two centuries of the white ruling class in America. It was all so clear, and it was still going on. His own industry had been as guilty as any in defaming the Indian, in perpetuating the lie. For the next two decades Brando would act, whenever he or they thought it useful, as the Indians' public advocate.

BIG STAR, SMALL FILMS

Brando's growing immersion in political activism was not reflected in his next few films. *Bedtime Story* was in fact his least political for some time, a typical Universal light comedy of the period, a situation farce complete with romantic overtones, featuring him and David Niven as two con-men preying on the fairer sex in Europe.

The two men got on well together. Brando later claimed that it was the only set on which he'd "really enjoyed" himself. Niven made him laugh so much that the two men "got the giggles like two girls at a boarding school . . . He finally had to ask me to go to my trailer, I couldn't stop laughing. We both thought it was such a funny script, such a funny story."

Niven himself noted that "contrary to what I had heard, Brando was easy, sympathetic and generous to work with." The British actor was certainly right for the film; there have been few actors in Hollywood's history more adept at playing this sort of role, and Brando's relative lack of a comic touch was more than compensated by Niven's mastery of his.

The story begins with the two men plying their trades on

different sides of the Alps. Niven's Lawrence prowls the Côte d'Azur in search of rich women to bed and fleece, whereas Brando's Freddy, an Army corporal stationed in Germany, goes from cottage to cottage telling frauleins that this is where his poor old granny used to live. He even has a photograph—taken moments before—to prove it. The fraulein, learning that he's such a sensitive man, naturally offers him bed and board for an hour or two.

Discharged, Freddy travels south in search of richer pickings and meets Lawrence on the train. They should work together, Freddy says, but Lawrence is not interested in the idea—not until Freddy blackmails him into it. As a team they pursue Lawrence's old game, with Freddy playing the mad brother who shows up in time to scare off the now-fleeced victim. Lawrence, however, is putting some of their ill-earned money into supporting the local arts, and when Freddy learns of this he's naturally appalled. They agree on a duel to decide who keeps the "territory"—whoever can get $25,000 out of soap queen Janet Walker will be the winner. But Freddy falls in love with her, and anyway she's as much of a fraud as they are . . .

Bedtime Story is reasonably entertaining in the usual facile manner. It's thoroughly sexist, but in 1963 films with good female parts could be counted on one thumb, and feminist films were virtually inconceivable. The one note of interest for the Brando-watcher was the choice of characterizations used by Freddy: they nearly all echo previous Brando roles—caricatures of Napoleon, Kowalski, Wilozek and Diestl punctuate the movie like a row of deflating myths. Just how deliberate this was remains unknown, but there seems no doubt that the more Brando became involved in the politics of the outside world the more he seemed to need to apologize for being an actor.

But even if he'd wanted to quit, he couldn't afford to. "Sometimes I need the money," he said with regard to his next project. It's like a car and an oil dipstick. You look at it once in a while, and you find you need oil. Well, every so often I look at my financial condition and I find I need money, so I do a good-paying picture. You see, I have three households to support and I pay

Between pages 112–113
Page 1: *The Wild One*
Page 2: *One-Eyed Jacks*
Page 3: top: *Mutiny on the Bounty;* bottom: *Queimada*
Page 4: *The Missouri Breaks*

alimony to two women." Plus, he realized that it was as a star that he could make the most political impact, as a rich star that he could afford to help the many who came to him in need of financial support for their worthy causes. The movies had to keep coming.

He was back in Christian Diestl territory for *The Saboteur: Code Name—Morituri,* playing another German caught up in the Second World War. There were also other links with his past career: Aaron Rosenberg was the producer and Trevor Howard one of his co-stars. The fact that both had agreed to work with him again so soon after *Mutiny* doesn't say much for the credibility of those who blamed all that picture's woes on his behavior.

The story has Crain (Brando), a wealthy German pacifist domiciled in India, blackmailed by British Intelligence (Howard) into accepting an undercover assignment aboard a German freighter carrying rubber home to the Fatherland. Since Crain is posing as a Gestapo-agent the ship's anti-Nazi captain (Yul Brynner) doesn't like him very much. On the other hand, the pro-Nazi First Officer (Martin Benrath) thinks him the best thing since sliced bockwurst. Everyone but Brando makes the appropriate grimaces, smirks, knowing looks, etc., beloved of routine melodrama. Brando, who is actually acting, looks out of place. Anyway, the Brits attack the Krauts, but the Nips attack the Brits, and then transfer Yank prisoners to the Kraut boat. The Yanks gang-rape a Jewish lady prisoner, Craine is unmasked, a mutiny breaks out and is quashed, Crain escapes . . .

While all this is going on Brando is playing a sort of German Terry Malloy, a man coming to terms with the conflicting priorities of survival and conscience. Daniel Taradash's script seems occasionally cognizant of the fact that two different films are being made, but the philosophical chunks he has inserted for Brando's character seem about as profound as the script he wrote for *Desirée.* The director, Bernhard Wicki, seems to have had his own ideas, and none of them involved discussing matters with his cast. The impression left behind is of a star too big for the film, of an exercise which has only served to demonstrate how easy it is to mislay talent on a German freighter. The only moral to be drawn was that any film needing both a colon and a dash in its title was beyond help.

The Chase had a notably brief title, and was consequently a rather superior offering. Brando had a better relationship with director Arthur Penn than he'd had with Wicki, but unfortunately Penn's relationships with the writers and producers could hardly have been worse. The cast was excellent—Brando, Jane Fonda, James Fox, Robert Redford, Angie Dickinson, E.G. Marshall, Janice Rule—and the basic idea was sound enough. The film is set in a small, southern town on one very hot Saturday night. A local boy has broken out of jail some miles away and is known to be heading homeward. Most of the people in the town are affected by this news in one way or another, and their reactions, as the night winds on, increasingly reveal the frustration of their lives and the corruption festering at the heart of the town's ruling family.

Penn says that the film was wrecked by the producers before release, but the finished product, though perhaps overblown, remains both convincing and gripping enough. It is recognizably a Penn film in its concentration on the fragility of civilization and the barbarism lurking just beneath the surface. It aims at the gut, and it hits the gut. Those critics who accused Penn of trying to do too much should have saved their spite for the directors who spend their lives getting away with doing too little.

Brando, playing the town sheriff, the guardian of the civilized crust, is the last to succumb to the mounting hysteria, and in this sense is the film's central tragic figure. If he's not immune, then who is? At the end he leaves the town a sadder man, bloody and barely unbowed.

Some critics noted a similarity between *The Chase* and *The Wild One,* and both, it's true, reek of the same, smalltown claustrophobia. Others added that Brando was now playing the "opposite" role, the nemesis of the wild ones, but it seems more pertinent to note that in both films he plays the rebel. In the latter film rebellion might consist of no more than respect for the rule of law, but America had come a long way since 1953.

Sheriff Calder was not a very demanding role, but as an actor Brando was still impressing people. Penn, unhappy with the

The saboteur

Overleaf: Up to his knees in melodrama, with Robert Redford in *The Chase*

script, asked him to improvise, and "he did it brilliantly . . . it was inarticulate and raw, but passionate." When all these scenes were cut out of the final version Penn called it "a great loss of some of the best acting I've ever witnessed."

Director Sidney J. Furie was not so impressed with Brando during the filming of *The Appaloosa* (*Southwest to Sonora* in UK). "He's disorganized," Furie complained. "No discipline at all. A procrastinator. One little scene that should have taken us a few hours took ten days." Brando, for his part, was no happier with his director, whose insistence on repeating the bizarre camera angles which had marked his *Ipcress File* success was a source of derisive amusement to most of the crew. "Furie's even shooting up the horse's ass" was one comment.

But the basic problem, as always, was the lack of a finished, coherent script. At the first meeting between star, director and screenwriter James Bridges, Brando had penciled out the twenty-five per cent of the movie which involved an Indian fight, and for the next four months sequences were written, re-written, de-written and re-re-written. Brando kept insisting that the finished product should help the Indian cause, but this was difficult to manage when the basic story, in co-star John Saxon's estimation, was "boy meets horse, boy loses horse, boy gets horse." Once again Brando was trying to get political capital out of a non-political account, and once he realized this his interest waned. When Saxon noticed this and good-heartedly threatened to "stel the picture" Brando replied "be my guest."

The Appaloosa looks at times like unshown portions of *One-Eyed Jacks,* with the star in his Mexican gear moving broodily from one violent scene to another across stretches of awe-inspiring landscape. There are fine moments; Saxon is suitably villainous, Anjanette Comer suitably enticing. But once more the overriding sensation is one of dissonance, as Brando's sheer presence and quality as an actor dwarf both the plot and the character he inhabits. It's watchable but it's also unsettling. For the third movie in a row he was too big for his film.

As Matt in *The Appaloosa*

FROM THE RIDICULOUS TO THE SUBLIME

Brando agreed to take the male lead in *A Countess from Hong Kong* "because Chaplin asked me. When a man of his stature in the industry writes a script for you, you can hardly refuse. Why he should think of me for comedy, I haven't the faintest idea. But he said I was the only one who could play it." As for the script, he read it, "then read it again, then tried reading it upside-down."

It became clear that he was playing an American named Ogden, "a man from an aristocratic family, well-dressed but wan, tired—not jaded, but archly bemused by the world at large. He is married and is trying for an important government post, an ambassadorship. No, maybe it's Secretary of State. The appointment comes through, and he gets himself involved with a semi-hooker, a White Russian. She stows away in his cabinet on an ocean liner, and he spends much of his time trying to keep her hidden."

In other words, a Whitehall farce, full of trouser-dropping, people hiding in cupboards and, given the oceanic setting, seasickness-sufferers in search of open portholes. The story had been thought up by Chaplin in the late thirties, and unfortunately it showed. The dialogue was laced with stale clichés, the characterizations were pure stereotypes. Before too long Brando "was wanting to go to Charlie and say 'I'm afraid we've made a terrible mistake.'"

But he didn't—his respect for the old Hollywood rebel was too great. Perhaps he was also awed by Chaplin's total self-confidence; the director didn't require his actors to act, only to duplicate the performances he demonstrated to them, scene by scene, line by line. As regards camera direction, working with Chaplin offered the ultimate contrast to Brando's recent experience with Furie. "I am the unusual and do not need camera angles," Chaplin had once exclaimed, and so it was.

Time had apparently stood still for the legend, and the film was

Dancing to Chaplin's tune in *A Countess from Hong Kong*

caught in his personal time warp. The critics said so, as tactfully as they could. For Brando, of all people, to have been caught up in this doomed project was simply bizarre.

Fortunately, he followed *Countess* with his best film of the decade. *Reflections in a Golden Eye* was taken from a Carson McCullers novella and directed by John Huston. The cast, as strong as that assembled for *The Chase,* included Liz Taylor, Julie Harris, Robert Forster and the much-underrated Brian Keith. Brando, explaining his reasons for taking the part, was typically self-effacing: "The appeal to me of a neurotic role like Major Pemberton? $750,000 plus seven and a half per cent of the gross receipts if we break even. That's the main reason . . . then the attraction of a book by Carson McCullers." After all, his recent parts had hardly been brimming with contemporary significance.

And Major Pemberton also posed an acting challenge. The story takes place on a U.S. Army post in the South, and the plot revolves around a complex network of unsatisfactory relationships. Pemberton's wife (Liz Taylor) is having an affair with Colonel Langdon (Keith), and his wife (Harris), a very troubled lady, is platonically involved with their Filipino houseboy. Pemberton himself is attracted to a private (Forster), and coming agonizingly to terms with his latent homosexuality. The private, of course, is besotted with Pemberton's wife. The scene is set for any number of tragic denouements, and most of them duly occur.

Brando's performance is quite extraordinary, one of the definitive screen portrayals of sexual repression. It is not so much the things he does—practicing with barbells, studying himself in the mirror, self-consciously applying his wife's rejuvenating cream—as the way he does them, the expressions on his face, the scowls that turn to smiles and back again, all the varied reflections of a man at odds with himself. The scene in which he whips the horse which has thrown him, simultaneously laughing and crying at his own reaction, should be compulsory viewing in drama schools.

Huston was amazed by the actor's talent. At Brando's suggestion one scene—a talk to new recruits—was shot three different ways, and Huston, finding each version perfect in its own terms, had

On the set of *Reflections in a Golden Eye* with (crouching) director John Huston

Overleaf: Major Pemberton

trouble deciding which to use. At last Brando had found a role and a film worthy of his talent, and though American reaction was mostly lukewarm, in Britain the film was highly praised.

But, as if to distance himself from a possible re-assertion of his previous status, he now made two movies which the world could well have done without. *Candy*, a soft porn satire on soft porn adapted from the novel by Terry Southern and Mason Hoffenberg, was the brainchild of Christian Marquand, a mediocre French actor-director who just happened to be an old friend of Brando. The latter agreed to play a cameo role, and this was enough to bring money rolling in. Once he'd persuaded Richard Burton to appear, other Hollywood names appended their signature to this dubious project.

Danish actress Ewa Aulin played the title role, moving from one sexual experience—or intended sexual experience—to the next with the assembled queue of luminaries. She ends up with Brando, playing Grindl, a guru who tours the States in a refrigerated truck complete with fitted temple and pool. It's a nice, superhammy study in cult assassination, and few people can have failed to realize that the Brando cult was one of its prime targets. The best line in the movie is saved for the end; it starts snowing inside the truck, Grindl is turned into a snowman, and the border cops archly announce that "you can't bring a frozen guru into California."

There's even less to say about *The Night of the Following Day*. Once more Brando was inveigled into a project by an old friend, in this case his ex-agent Jay Kanter, who was now heading MCA's British operations. The director was Hubert Cornfield, but he got on so badly with Brando and co-star Richard Boone, that the latter replaced him for the last fortnight of filming.

The film is a "contemporary" low-budget thriller. An heiress (Pamela Franklin) is collected by a chauffeur on arrival in Paris and delivered to his partners-in-kidnapping. Once ensconced in a remote beach cottage the usual intra-gang tensions—personal dislikes, ransom logistics, escape attempts and one's attitude towards them—are spiced with sexual sadism (the "contemporary" bit) and eventually resolved in the obligatory, violent fashion. The "chauffeur" survives his partners, goes back for the abused heiress,

Grindl levitates himself, but he can't lift *Candy*

Overleaf: The calendar says it all. (*The Night of the Following Day*)

who then opens her eyes to find she's arriving on a plane in Paris. There's a chauffeur waiting. Dream or premonition? Neat, eh?

Boone is lovably nasty as the aptly-named Leer, and Brando is convincing enough as nobody in particular. Shipman thought it "his least rewarding work since he entered films," Paulene Kael thought Brando had never "been worse or less interesting." It was an all-too-fitting footnote to his work over the previous decade.

BURNED

Perhaps a revival was at hand; Hollywood was suddenly buzzing with the news that Brando had signed to work with Kazan once more on *The Arrangement,* fifteen years on from their last mutual success with *On the Waterfront.* The actor was also said to be wanted by Twentieth Century-Fox, to partner Paul Newman in a western with smash written all over it, *Butch Cassidy and the Sundance Kid.* But, luckily for Robert Redford, Fox couldn't get an answer from Brando, couldn't even find him. Far from the corporate boardrooms, something of rather greater significance had taken place.

On April 4, 1968, Martin Luther King had been shot dead in Memphis, and Brando, who had spoken with the civil rights leader only weeks before, was devastated by the news. His next public appearance, a week later, was at the funeral of Black Panther Bobby Hutton in Oakland. Kazan was told that the reunion was off: Brando would be too busy with his political work.

Or, as it turned out, a hard-hitting political film. He had met Gillo Pontecorvo, the director of *The Battle of Algiers,* while in Rome for *Candy,* and the Italian had shown him the script for what was eventually to become *Queimada (Burn* in the U.S.). Brando had liked it, but had not committed himself. Now, it seems, the urge to make such a film was stronger.

Pontecorvo, for his part, wanted the American for two reasons. The first was financial—with Brando's name attached to the project he could hope for Hollywood money. The second was artistic. "When Solinas and I began to construct the script," he said, "we had three actors in mind: Lancaster, Burton and Brando. But, as the story grew, we decided that the only one who could do this role was Brando. There are many moments when there is no time for dialogue, and then we need the synthesis of Brando's acting and his face. When things are psychological, we trust the face of Brando."

But did Brando trust the cinema of Pontecorvo? *Queimada* was a new experience for him, and one that would crystallize many of the difficulties confronting a politically-minded Hollywood actor who wanted to make political movies. For a start, he'd have to leave Hollywood, to work with—under might be a better word—one of the *engagé* European directors. These latter were not generally noted for their willingness to share control over the film-making process, and Pontecorvo was no exception to the norm. "American film actors are spoilt," he said around this time. "Just because they are often good, they think it gives them the right to interfere where no one has asked them to interfere . . . For the European director the actor is a collaborator who may be extraordinary and even decisive for the realization of his work as he conceives it, but the actor must fit into the idea that the author has . . . an actor can give himself enough space in which to express his own personality and temperament within the framework of a film that remains the product of a single person."

So much for collectivism. Apparently, socialist films could only be made in a feudalistic style reminiscent of the old Hollywood. Apparently also, companies making such films full of third-world-liberation fervor were prepared to pay black extras less than white extras if they could get away with it. And as for the horses, well, they weren't mentioned in the revolutionary texts.

Brando objected on all these counts, and as regards the extras and the horses was able to improve matters. But he and Pontecorvo had an uneasy relationship, both full of respect for the other's previous work, both deeply suspicious of the other's compatibility as a working partner. Pontecorvo, while thinking that Brando "can give more than it is possible for an actor to give," didn't think that "any artist should be so difficult." The actor didn't criticize the director in public, but his feelings—doubtless exacerbated by the appalling Colombian conditions under which the film was being made—were hardly a secret. With others, however, he was as helpful and considerate as ever. Evaristo Marquez, the black Colombian with no acting experience who'd been chosen to play the second lead, had every reason to be grateful. As Pontecorvo said: "Brando was so patient, coaxing Evaristo along, making faces, miming everything for him—what a drama coach!"

The story . . . well, imagine Lenin exiled from Russia by Stalin and forced to make his living as a Hollywood scriptwriter . . . the studio boss comes into his office . . . "Vladimir Ilych, we need you to re-write this *Captain Blood* script in a hurry; Errol wants more bite in it" . . . Lenin hurries to the screening-room and absorbs twelve straight hours of Hollywood swashbuckledom . . . later that evening, in his Malibu beach hut, he re-reads his own master-work, *Imperialism* . . .

Queimada is a Marxist adventure-story. It begins with the arrival of Sir William Walker (Brando), a sort of Victorian MI6 man, in the Portuguese Caribbean colony of Queimada; his mission is to break the Portuguese sugar monopoly and so ensure that the British have ample sugar for their Indian tea. He means to achieve his end by instigating a slave revolt against the colonial power, which sounds pretty cynical, but in fact he honestly believes that the interests of the slaves and the British coincide at this point in time. They will get their freedom, become wage-slaves rather than mere slaves, and Britain will get its sugar.

He tricks a young black, José Dolores (Evaristo Marquez), into becoming a wanted man, and then encourages him to lead a revolutionary struggle. At the same time he grooms an educated liberal, Sanchez (Renato Salvatore), for the power that Dolores' eventual victory brings. The latter becomes painfully aware of his ignorance when it comes to economics, and is persuaded to resign. Sanchez takes over and Sir William, a job well done, departs for "a place called Indochina."

Ten years later Sir William is found brawling in some proletarian den of iniquity by representatives of the British Royal

In thoughtful mood on the set of *The Night of the Following Day*

Overleaf: Sir William Walker and his liberal stooge. With Renato Salvatore in *Queimada*

Sugar Company. José Dolores, it seems, is on the march once more, and the company want him to return to Queimada and set things right.

But the Sir William who returns is not the man who left. "Ten years," as he says, "is a long time, a very long time. Between one historical period and another ten years might be enough to reveal the contradictions of a whole century . . . we have to realize that our judgment and our interpretations and . . . even our hopes may have been wrong . . . my ideas at the moment are concerned with how to get some things done, not with why to do it."

In other words, the interests of the slaves and the British no longer coincide, and he knows it. The revolutions of 1848 have failed in Europe, and Sir William now realizes that a mode of production's gotta do what a mode of production's gotta do. Which in this case is to crush José Dolores. He sets to the task with fire and sword.

Dolores is caught, and Sir William tries to explain that this just wasn't the time. He tries to do a deal with his erstwhile protégé, even offers to help him escape, but the revolutionary prefers the purity of a martyr's death. He knows superior power when he sees it, but he doesn't accept that Sir William's "historical inevitability" obviates the need for the making of moral choices. He dies on the scaffold; Sir William, with rather less dignity, is stabbed to death as he prepares to leave the island.

One problem with *Queimada* is apparent from this synopsis of the script. Any film about a popular uprising and its suppression which can be summed up in terms of three characters obviously distorts the events it seeks to portray. This is not Pontecorvo's fault, it is inherent in the project itself. Just as historians tend to recount events either in terms of personalities or whole classes, so political movies seem destined to end up as either heavily individualized or heavily didactic.

In *The Battle of Algiers* Pontecorvo managed to alleviate this problem by using unknown faces, but in *Queimada* he exacerbates matters by using Brando. George Melly noted that the star's face was too well-known, and that this familiarity "partially destroys the sense of *cinema verité* which is Pontecorvo's main strength."

A pyrrhic victory. Sir William takes in the defeated José Dolores. With Evaristo Marquez in *Queimada*

Overleaf: A temporary setback for Royal Sugar

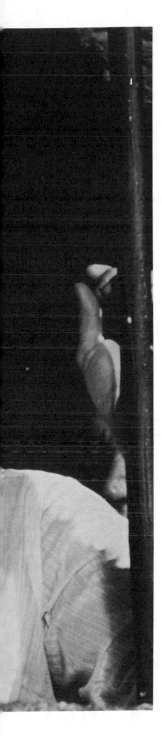

But it is not so much Brando's face as his eye-catching talent. He makes Sir William so interesting, so aware, so watchable, that the balance of the picture in a political sense is lost. *Queimada* becomes more of an exercise in European revolutionary masochism than a tale of Third World liberation.

This should not be overstated. The amount of emotional space given to the real victims of European/American arrogance in *Queimada* far exceeds that allowed the Vietnamese in films like *Coming Home* and *The Deer Hunter*. And the film has many admirable qualities. It's splendid spectacle; few other living directors know how to use crowds as well as Pontecorvo, or share his ability to make cinematic sense of chaotic violence. There are moments of heart-wrenching agony; at times it seems as if the whole shameful history of white behavior in the Third World has been compressed into a single, accusative frame. Morricone's music is, as always, near-perfect.

Above all, *Queimada,* as a "Marxist adventure story," tells a story that needs to be told in an accessible way. Its ideological structure is perhaps over-schematic, but Marx once defended his emphasis on economic factors on the grounds that everyone else was busy de-emphasizing them, and Pontecorvo could certainly make similar claims. After decades of watching Errol Flynn tweaking the noses of silly, fat colonial governors, it's nice to see for once just what and who they represented, just how wide and how deep was the network of corruption and human misery underlying their fat silliness.

PART 4
TALES OF VANISHED POWER

The Nightcomers

The Godfather

Last Tango in Paris

NC-3

HEROES AND VILLAINS

Queimada was not a commercial success; mixed reviews and a less than enthusiastic promotion effort doomed it to the art cinema circuit and a fairly swift TV sale. To many it seemed just one more proof of Brando's inability to recapture the focus of his career, one more eccentric twist in a downward spiral. Soon he wouldn't be worth criticizing.

The Godfather changed all that; suddenly all the people who'd been lamenting his inevitable eclipse were basking in the light of his "comeback." No attempt was made to explain this comeback, any more than any real attempt had been made to explain the trumpeted decline. *The Godfather* was a lucky break, they said, a good film by any standard, Brando had finally come to his senses and returned to Hollywood basics. He was, after all, America's finest actor. Hadn't they said so all along?

But *The Godfather* was much more than a lucky break, and the revival in Brando's fortunes was no accident. Both were signs of the changing times, reflecting changes in the society at large and the film industry in particular. The sixties were over. The scream of rage had turned into the enduring murmur of discontent; the prime concern now—to turn Marx on his head—was not to change society but to interpret it. So much that had seemed possible had failed to occur, and the desires unleashed by the sixties' mental leap into the future were now channelled into the mental wringing of hands. The cultural bandwagon set in motion by the political events of the last decade continued to roll, even though the politics themselves had come to little more than might-have-beens. What was no longer expressed on the streets was still being expressed in books, on record, and on the theater screen.

Hollywood too had been infected by the virus of change. The structure of the industry was being transformed, at the bottom by the spread of independent companies, at the top by the absorption of the whole film-producing business into the giant transnational corporations. The audience was changing too; the old mass market

Previous page: A typical Michael Winner composition from *The Nightcomers*

As Quint in *The Nightcomers*

stolen by TV had been replaced, after a decade of near panic, by a new, discriminatory and overwhelmingly young audience, eager for films which reflected its view of the world, its fantasies and realities. And to provide these films a new generation of writers and directors was emerging, men and women who had served their apprenticeships in the sixties, who understood only too well the sense of blocked catharsis which would dominate the seventies.

For the leading men and women who would star in their films, all this implied a change of approach. The sort of stories they would be offered, the sort of directors they would work with, would be profoundly different. The old Hollywood movie, complete with hero and heroine fighting the good fights and ending up in church together, was now fit only for TV. At the theater reality was expected, if only in terms of noticeable exit wounds.

For the actresses these changes were a mixed blessing. They would find themselves required to bare more than their souls, but they would also find, as the decade wore on, that real parts were being written for women. Indeed, the "woman-alone-in-a-patriarchal-world" would, for a short time, become the only clear-cut heroism Hollywood had to offer.

For the leading man things were more problematic. The Cary Grant-figure had not survived Vietnam as a serious protagonist, and was consequently relegated to the two genres—romantic comedy and science fiction—which no one but the kids took too seriously. The new heroes came in two basic forms. The first of these, the establishment renegade, only differed from the old hero in one fundamental way—he realized that the men at the top were as wicked as the men at the bottom. So he could be anti-establishment and anti- the normal nasties, a political position which allowed him to double the number of people he could sneer at or shoot. The second new hero was a truer reflection of contemporary society, a man uncertain of everything but the corruption of the establishment. He knew he couldn't win in a political sense, but he could try and make sense of his own life, and be witty in the process.

And, of course, for the second leading men there were the

Previous page: Making offers that can't be refused. As Don Vito Corleone in *The Godfather*

establishment figures whom the first leading men were sneering at. They could be new-style villains of all kinds, ranging from bent San Franciscan cops to lords of evil empires like Darth Vader.

At first sight, none of this seemed very promising as far as Brando was concerned. Neither of the new hero-figures suited him. The first was clearly a right-wing fantasy, and equally clearly offered little in the way of an acting challenge. You could happily forget that Eastwood and Bronson were and are good actors, because it's years since they've needed to demonstrate their skill. The second, in reflecting youthful uncertainty, seemed ill-fitted to a man who was neither youthful nor, personal terms excepted, uncertain. The only time Brando was to stray into this territory— of which Nicholson was undoubtedly the king—was in *Last Tango in Paris,* a film which dealt exclusively with the personal realm.

Unable to play heroic figures, Brando chose to play members of the bankrupt establishment. Sir William Walker was not so much the end of one career as the beginning of another, the first of five major parts through which Brando would explore the face and the soul of contemporary evil, creating a portfolio of corruption as human as it was corrupt, a reflection of the seventies as powerfully apposite as his earlier reflection of the repressed fifties.

THE SUCCESSFUL AMERICAN

The Godfather saga began when Mario Puzo decided that he was fed up with being poor. Writing good books didn't pay, so he'd do one that was half-good, on a subject which looked commercial— the Mafia. He started it in 1965, and three years later the saga of the Corleone family was finished. Puzo wouldn't be poor much longer.

Despite growing indications of the book's eventual success, Paramount, which had prudently acquired the film rights, was in no great rush to make the film. Another Mafia movie, *The Brotherhood,* had recently flopped, and the company tried to hedge

Overleaf:
American businessmen, one and all

its bets by arranging a co-production deal with Dino de Laurentiis. Charles Bronson would star. But this deal fell through—Laurentiis and Bronson went on to make their own Mafia movie *The Valachi Papers*—and Paramount were left holding their half-wanted baby.

The production top brass, Bob Evans and Peter Bart, were not interested in producing the film themselves, so they handed the chore to Albert Ruddy, whose previous screen career was hardly littered with smashes. The budget would be small, and things like period recreation would not be possible. At this stage everyone was looking for a cheap gangster movie that could cash in on the book's success.

They didn't need an expensive director for such a film, and once Richard Brooks and Costa-Gavras had turned the assignment down, the little-known figure of Francis Ford Coppola was suggested by Bart. His previous films—*You're a Big Boy Now, Finian's Rainbow* and *The Rain People*—had pleased the critics more than the public, but Coppola was known to bring in his films on time and within a budget. Being young and in need of a commercial success, he might be easier to control than a bigger name. For his part, Coppola was none too keen on the subject-matter, but the company he and George Lucas ran had cash-flow problems—i.e. they were broke—and a paying job was a paying job. He accepted.

Now the arguments began. Don Corleone, the head of the story's central family, was clearly the key role to cast, and Puzo, who was to co-write the screenplay with Coppola, had already sent a copy of the novel to Brando. The actor didn't bother to read it; Paramount, he told Puzo, would never hired him anyway. Coppola, however, agreed with Puzo that an actor of Brando's stature (and in his view that meant the man himself or Olivier) had to play Don Corleone. He told Ruddy so, but the producer shared Brando's opinion of the likely top-brass reaction. He bet Coppola $200 that they would never accept him in the role.

But Coppola was not dissuaded, and his first task was to get Brando interested. They talked, and the actor read the book. It was, he thought, a significant piece of social comment, an allegory of the corporate mentality in America.

Armed with Brando's yes, Coppola entered the lions' den. The lions duly roared. Evans shouted at him for his idiocy; Jaffe, the company president, told Coppola, "I assure you that Marlon Brando will never appear in this motion picture and, furthermore, as President of the company, I will no longer allow you to discuss it." Coppola continued discussing it, explaining why the actor was so right for the part and, more to the corporate point, suggesting ways of insuring the company against another *Mutiny*-style fiasco. Brando would test for the role, would put up a bond against personal misbehavior, and would receive no salary, only a share of the profits. And despite their misgivings, Jaffe and Evans gave way.

Coppola went back to Brando, anxiously wondering how he could persuade a legend to audition for him. But the actor had already been thinking about voice and make-up, and with tissues stuck inside his cheeks gave an impromptu performance for Coppola's camera. This was shown to the Paramount executives, who didn't realize at first who it was they were watching. Whomever it was seemed perfect. Brando had the part.

The arguments continued, with the casting of Michael Corleone a particular source of contention. The executives wanted Warren Beatty, but Coppola insisted that only Al Pacino could do justice to the role. If Paramount had wanted a director they could order around, then they'd picked the wrong one. Meanwhile the book was selling even better than expected, and as its sales went up the film's projected budget followed suit. The potboiler was slowly turning into something with class.

While the arguments raged on, Brando was in England, filming *The Nightcomers* with Michael Winner. He wasn't receiving any salary for this movie either, because even armed with Brando's name, Winner had been hard-pushed to raise the finance needed for shooting. The film would offer a fictional account of the events leading up to those narrated in Henry James' equally fictional *Turn of the Screw,* and Brando had been drawn to the project by two familiar factors, his friendship for Jay Kanter and an interest in the possibilities of his role, the working-class Irish gardener Quint. In *The Nightcomers* it is the latter's tortured sex-affair with

'We're not murderers, no matter what the undertaker says'

the children's governess which creates James' unexplained traumas.

It was a good role, and Brando was as convincing as ever, but the overall product was spoiled by Winner's penchant for karate-style editing and his love for the zoom lens. This style of movie-making would work well in Winner's above-par action movies like *Lawman, Chato's Land* and *Death Wish,* but here they served only to de-intensify what should have been a claustrophobic atmosphere. Both Brando and Winner enjoyed working together, but the film didn't set any box offices on fire.

While Brando was working on *The Nightcomers,* Coppola stayed in Cambridge with him, writing by day and discussing Don Corleone with Brando in the evenings. The actor was fully involved in the business of defining his character, and listened with interest to the tapes Coppola had brought with him of the Kefauver Investigation into Organized Crime proceedings. One voice, that of Frank Costello, struck both men as ideal for Don Corleone.

Back in the States, filming began early in 1971. It was Brando's first work in his own country since *The Appaloosa* six years before (excepting a few location shots for *Reflections in a Golden Eye*), but if he was nervous it didn't show. According to James Caan, playing the Don's number one son, "the pressure was incredible. Paramount acted like it was the first movie ever being made. And do you know who was the greatest tension reliever of all? Brando. The guy was fantastic." As usual he helped out the least experienced actor, in this case Al Martino, coaxing him, encouraging him, occasionally resorting to subterfuge. During the shooting of one scene he slapped Martino twice as hard as the singer was expecting, and the look of pained surprise he received was exactly what the director ordered.

But the man who most needed his help was Coppola. Paramount had given in to most of the director's demands so far, but the film had assumed an importance far in excess of that originally intended. It was now a big project, and Coppola's inexperience in handling such projects was soon in evidence. Rumors that he would be dumped in favor of Kazan or Avakian were spreading.

Some members of his crew were not as supportive as they should have been. Brando, however, stuck with the young director, and his promise to follow Coppola off the picture perhaps helped to persuade the Paramount executives against replacing him. The tide once turned, Coppola sacked some of the crew and got down to making one of the best movies of the decade.

The Godfather traces ten years (1945–55) in the history of the Sicilian-American Corleone family, one of the "five families" who control organized crime in the U.S. from their New York bases. Throughout the movie the accent is on both the family and their "business," and the opening half-hour is used to illustrate the schizophrenic nature of their life, switching from the sunlit wedding reception to the dark rooms where the head of the family, Don Vito Corleone, makes people "offers they can't refuse."

Trouble soon arrives: the other four families are keen to get in on the growing and lucrative drug market, but Don Corleone opts out, afraid he'll antagonize his political connections if he gets involved in such an unsavory business. This decision is not accepted by his putative partners, who decide that Sonny (James Caan), his heir apparent, will be more amenable. But the Don survives the attempted assassination, and it is Sonny who is eventually cut to ribbons. His death brings the other main theme to the fore: the position of younger brother Michael (Al Pacino), who's been college-educated and apparently destined for better things. The Don, in a speech with ironic echoes of the *Waterfront* taxi conversation, says that he's always expected Michael to become a senator or something, but Michael is caught by family and fate, and when the Don eventually dies he is ready to step into his shoes, to become the new Godfather.

It's a fairly simple story, flawlessly acted amidst a near-perfect recreation of the period in question. Brando dominates the movie, despite being off-screen for more than half its length; his characterization of Don Corleone gives the story its moral complexity and thus its power as a document of human drama. He is fearsome yet oddly pathetic, the ultimate realist locked in by history, he is real from the minutiae of accent and gestures to the aura of ambiguity which his personality radiates. We are here in

Overleaf: Don Corleone and his reluctant heir. With Al Pacino in *The Godfather*

the presence of evil and in the presence of innocence, and no matter how hard we insist that the two cannot co-exist in the same cinematic character, the figure of Don Corleone proves that they can.

The movie had its share of criticism. Robert K. Johnston, in his *Francis Ford Coppola,* thought that the film's portrait of the Mafia—they were not called that in the script, thanks to pressure from Italian-American pressure groups—was unrealistic. The real Mafia families, he argued, were more repressive, more prone to mutual disloyalty, and much less likely to turn down a slice of the drug business. While welcoming the accent on family life, Johnston deplored the portrayal of the women, relegated to mere appendages of male society, shallow and without importance. Shipman, criticizing Coppola's and Brando's claims of the movie's social significance (see below), thought there was "no message and no moral." Andrew Sarris, writing in *Sight and Sound,* went further: he thought *The Godfather* was "about as unkind to the Mafia as *Mein Kampf* is to Adolf Hitler."

All of which was to miss the point. Coppola and Brando were not interested in mounting an attack on organized crime, nor in apologizing for it. To have tried to paint one side good and the other evil would have destroyed the movie. This was the seventies, and the certainty of good and evil was lacking. That was the point. Paulene Kael, as so often, hit it on the nose: "When Americanism was a form of cheerful, bland official optimism, the gangster used to be destroyed at the end of the movie . . . Now the whole mood of the country has darkened, guiltily." She pointed out that "Terry Malloy didn't clean up the docks," even though *Waterfront* ended as if he could, as if he had. *The Godfather,* by contrast, made no such spurious claims to a happy ending. It expressed the "new tragic realism."

This might not have been what Coppola and Brando had been aiming for, but it's certainly what they achieved. All the themes of the film are part and parcel of this "tragic realism." At the most superficial level the gangsters are de-romanticized figures, unable to sustain an audience on the level of gratuitous fantasy. At the "family level," the slow drawing of Michael into the corrupt world

An old man, innocent and evil

made by his father is a door slammed on the future, while the "new
business methods" he is forced to employ are a door slammed on
the past. As Stephen Farber observed, the immigrant generation
"tried to bring a measure of personal feeling into everything they

In the flat that
Paul built

did . . . but in a streamlined corporate America, all transactions are impersonal."

At the political level *The Godfather* attempts, and in large parts succeeds, in making the connection between organized crime and organized business. As Coppola said: "Both the Mafia and America have roots in Europe . . . Basically, both the Mafia and America feel they are benevolent organizations. Both the Mafia and America have their hands stained with blood from what it is necessary to do to protect their power and interests. Both are totally capitalistic phenomena and basically have a profit motive."

Brando expanded on this, adding that if the Mafia "had been black or socialist, Corleone would have been dead or in jail. But because the Mafia patterned itself so closely on the corporation, and dealt in a hard-nosed way with money, and with politics, it prospered. The Mafia is so . . . *American.* To me a key phrase in the story is that whenever they wanted to kill somebody it was always a matter of policy. Just before pulling the trigger they told him: "Just business. Nothing personal." When I read that, MacNamara, Johnson and Rusk flashed before my eyes."

And yes, it is easy to take the sunny world where the women and children "play" as Disneyland, the dark rooms where the decisions are taken as the war-rooms of the Pentagon. At root *The Godfather* is about America, and like no other film it manages to evoke both the innocence and the evil which that country reflects, the amazing creativity and the apparently depthless corruption of the spirit which seem the dual inheritance of profit-worship. Don Corleone personifies the ambivalence. He dies playing with his grandchild, orange-rind fangs stuck between his lips, the monster-in-fun strangely at ease with the real monster within.

LAST DANCE

In the summer of 1971, his work on *The Godfather* completed, Brando spent some time in Paris. There he met Bernardo

Bertolucci, the Italian director whom many considered the rising star of the European cinema. Brando had heard good reports of *The Conformist* and he liked Bertolucci; both men were idealistically-inclined veterans of psycho-analysis, and they shared a similar vision of the cinema's place in the world.

The Italian was working on the screenplay for what would become *Last Tango in Paris,* and had just heard that his intended male lead, Jean-Louis Trintignant, would not after all be available. He explained the basic idea to Brando, who was interested. He also approved of Bertolucci's approach to the director-actor relationship, his idea that the actor was a "co-author."

Brando hadn't had many such relationships with directors, and he agreed to fill Trintignant's place. But first he was scheduled to make *Child's Play,* a story of strange goings-on in an American private school. Or at least, that was what producer David Merrick intended it to be. Brando, according to one report, demanded that the school be turned into an orphanage, and that his old friend Wally Cox be given one of the parts. He threatened to mumble if his demands weren't met, but Merrick then countered by threatening to have his voice dubbed by John Wayne. It was a nice story, and possibly true. Either way, *Child's Play* and Brando parted company, and Robert Preston was brought in to take his role. The film turned out watchably dreadful.

Getting back to Bertolucci must have been refreshing, and the director made it plain from the start that Brando's contributions would be as crucial as his own. In fact, the character in the screenplay was fast becoming Brando, for the simple reason that Bertolucci found Brando more interesting. "I had at my disposal," he said, "two alternatives: one was the great actor, with all the technical experience that any director would require; the second was a mysterious man who was waiting there to be discovered in all the richness of his material. It was like leaving for an adventurous journey with two or three spare tires in the trunk of your car. If one of the tires blew out, I always had a spare. But I never used it."

Brando himself, according to the director, was "hunting for all the secrets he had hidden in all of his films. He loved and hated improvising his scenes. He loved it because it was new for him and

An American in Paris. As Paul in *Last Tango*

Overleaf: A rare excursion into the outside world. With Jeanne (Maria Schneider) peeking over Paul's shoulder

hated it because it seemed a violation of his privacy." The actor agreed. "Never again will I make a film like this one," he said. "For the first time, I have felt a violation of my innermost self. It should be the last time."

Last Tango begins with two strangers, Paul (Brando) and Jeanne (Maria Schneider), meeting in an empty apartment-to-let. Living-space is obviously not the only thing they each need: within minutes they're making sex up against a convenient wall. Paul takes the apartment and they agree to go on meeting there, for sex and sex only. No names, no history, Paul tells her.

Jeanne is initially stunned/captivated by Paul's physical directness, and when we meet her fiancé Tom (Jean-Pierre Leaud), a spoof-Godard who only seems interested in her as a camera-object, we begin to understand why. She's also, it turns out, the daughter of a dead colonel with a cupboard full of medals, the repressed French bourgeoisie *par excellence*. Paul is not something in her previous terms of reference.

He's an American whose wife has just died, he's a flophouse owner, and he's Brando. The stories of Paul's past, when they eventually come to be told, are Brando stories. Like Terry Malloy he's an ex-boxer, like Zapata he's been a revolutionary. Like Brando he's played the bongo-drums, and chased an ideal of women "through Africa, Asia and Indonesia." He talks about drunken parents on the family farm, the flophouse maid makes a passing remark about Tahiti. "Maybe it's not true," he muses, "maybe . . ."

At first he seems simply to want to use the girl, to let out his aggression on her, to degrade her to the ultimate degree. But it's he who starts relaxing his own rules for the relationship, who begins to talk personal history, to raise the spectre of interpersonal communication that transcends the purely sexual. We see him visit his dead wife's lover, the two of them sitting there in the identical bathrobes she bought for them. He can't understand how he lost her; at the funeral parlor he shouts abuse at her corpse, spilling his anguish, before tenderly wiping some of the thick make-up from her face. Perhaps this time, you can almost hear him thinking, I'll work it out better.

Meanwhile, Jeanne's wedding approaches, and as the initial spell is broken by his admission of growing involvement, she begins to see him less as an act of eros and more as an ageing romantic who owns a flophouse. He refuses to let her go, and after a last drunken conversation in a ballroom, follows her home. She, unable to control the situation any longer, shoots him with her father's revolver. "I didn't know him," she mutters, rehearsing her story for the police.

Needless to say, most of the publicity surrounding the film centered on the explicitness of the sex. The scene in which he sodomizes her with a little help from the butter-dish was discussed with relish. But, in truth, the sex on display is not particularly explicit, even by 1972 standards: much more of Brando's body had been on show in *The Nightcomers*. What is different is the emotional impact which the sexual scenes carry; *Last Tango*, as Paulene Kael observed in one of the most flattering film reviews she'd ever written, is a film in which "the sex expresses the characters' drives." One might say, expresses their lives.

Of course, this cut no ice with Disgusted of Tunbridge Wells or Appalled of Baton Rouge, both of whom considered butter as something one ate, preferably off a plate. But they weren't likely to see the film anyway.

There were more pertinent criticisms. Judith Crist thought the film "all machismo, filled with such detestation of and contempt for women that is universality is limited." David Shipman attacked on a broader front, finding fault with the dialogue ("all the scintillation and wit of the monologues in lesser Godard"), the end ("a cop-out"), the use of hack cinematic devices (the cut from sex-play to ducks in a pond, Paul's fondling of a razor, etc.), its reputation for sexual candor ("no one who saw it considered it erotic"), and, in particular, the sodomy and funeral parlor scenes. "You wonder that grown people can offer it as entertainment," he wrote, "or a comment on human behavior or whatever . . . the two scenes together make up the most repellently misogynist sequence of any movie yet made."

This was like blaming Hitchcock for Janet Leigh's murder in *Psycho*, like blaming historians for history. Most of the alleged faults were integral parts of the film intended. The dialogue is supposed to be real, the conversations of an ordinary man and girl, not literature. The end was a cop-out for the characters, not the film. The misogyny was the character's not the film's, and he duly pays for it. And, above all, *Last Tango* was not designed as an exercise in titillation, a come-on for the joys of sex. Eroticism, sexual love, is the film's messenger, not its message.

Last Tango is about pain, non-fulfillment, non-comprehension in personal relationships. Bertolucci wanted it to face the question: "Can a man and a woman still live together without destroying each other?," and he offered a topical answer. Paul/Brando, and by implication many others, seek a last chance of redemption in desire untrammelled by history, by one's own past or the other's extra-sexual reality. And it doesn't work, can't work, for more than a limited period of time. The girl realizes this, and she has another world waiting for her, but Paul finds himself driven to re-admit his own past and feelings, in both their negative (aggressive) and positive (romantic) aspects. Which of course dooms him to a re-run of past disappointments.

But, the film makes clear, he's not an extraordinary man. It's not his tragedy and his alone. When life is alienated, sex will be alienated sooner or later; life cannot be locked out of sex for more than a few days. Passion, by its very nature, is a transient phenomenon. As the woman at the tango competition tells Paul, "it" has nothing to do with love, it's a contest.

Paradoxically, the universality of the film's tragic theme is made all the more apparent by the presence of a very particular actor. As Kael observes: "If Brando knows this hell, why should we pretend we don't?" Here he is, the legend, the contemporary male hero, the man who did much to set the rebellion against sexual repression underway in the fifties, at the end of his emotional tether. In a curious way *Last Tango* and *The Godfather*, Paul and Don Corleone, complement each other, add up to a vision of humanity at a particular historical moment. The one reveals the political view, the other the emotional. As the character of Don Corleone expresses the emptiness of the good-evil, us-them notions of both an earlier Hollywood and the "revolutionary" sixties, so the

Previous page:
Collapse of the last tango

Pain and loneliness

character of Paul deflates the myth of sexual liberation as an answer in itself. Together they announced the seventies as a decade of shattered illusions.

A RAISED FINGER

Six months after the U.S. opening of *Last Tango* Brando was awarded the Best Actor Oscar for his portrayal of Don Corleone. He did not attend the ceremony, but sent an Apache actress, Sasheen Littlefeather, to reject the award on his behalf. The reason given was Hollywood's treatment of the American Indian.

No one, it seems, admired the gesture, but then "no one" probably didn't include many American Indians. Perhaps he should have rejected the award in person, perhaps not. Anyway, he had gained publicity for the cause closest to his heart, and everyone in Hollywood knew that any publicity was good publicity.

There was also, perhaps, another reason for his rejection. Perhaps Brando, thinking back to the Oscar which crowned his first run of success, decided that he didn't want a second round as a "hot" Hollywood "property," didn't want to be a "film star" again. To accept the Oscar might seem like a legitimization of Hollywood's version of his career, an acceptance of the terms which the film capital used to measure success in life. Everyone was talking about the great comeback, as if all his political work in the sixties had been a way of marking time between hit movies. This was not how Brando saw things, it never had been.

PART 5
"CHARLIE DON'T SURF"

The Missouri Breaks

Superman

Apocalypse Now

The Formula

COMMUTING FROM PARADISE

One of the many versions of the concluding section of *Mutiny on the Bounty* had been written by Brando himself. If featured Fletcher Christian sitting alone in a cave, silently contemplating man's perennial inhumanity to man, while elsewhere on the island his co-mutineers were unthinkingly blowing their chances of paradise. Brando had, in the words of one startled executive, written himself out of the movie, and not surprisingly this version was never shot, let alone printed.

In real life, though, the star could write himself out of movies, and the paradisial Tahiti seemed an ideal "cave" to write himself into. His local-law marriage to *Mutiny* co-star Tarita, and the birth of their two children, made Brando eligible to buy land in the area, and in the mid-sixties he acquired a group of islands, the largest of which, Tetiaroa, comprised some 450 acres.

He had two purposes in making the acquisition. Tetiaroa would provide him with the sort of privacy which he hungered for, and which even an armed compound in Hollywood could not provide. There he could enjoy the company of his children without a constant barrage of flashbulbs. He could read, walk naked on the beach, go out in his boat, simply float amidst the beauty of the unspoilt earth. On Tetiaroa, he said, he was "never bored or lonely."

But paradise was under threat, and not just for him. Brando's second purpose was to use Tetiaroa as a laboratory, a testing-ground for alternatives to the relentless spread of a spoiling civilization. It had all been "said well in *Future Shock*." The problems were "planetary . . . the same pollution . . . the same energy shortage . . . And we all seem to be at the mercy of these strange new countries that have been formed which are called international cartels . . . the multi-national companies that have no loyalty to anyone or responsibility to anyone . . ." By 1976 he was "convinced the world is doomed. The end is near. I wanted a place where my family and I could be self-sufficient and survive."

Previous page:
Jorel delivers sentence on a trio of galactic saboteurs in *Superman*

With Jack Nicholson and Arthur Penn on the set of *The Missouri Breaks*

He was also interested in more than himself and his family. If, Brando reasoned, he could use his money to investigate alternative energy and food sources, could show Tahiti ways of making itself more self-sufficient, then the ravages of commercial civilization might at least be postponed. He wanted to explore the possibilities of converting waste products to energy, to try out methods of utilizing solar power, of developing plankton as a food for humans. And he would do what he could to weaken the influence of his own country. He didn't think he'd let his children by Tarita go to the States. "As Tahitians, they are too trusting. They would be destroyed by the pace of life in the States."

All the intended scientific experiments would involve a great deal of expense, and Brando had never been noted for a propensity to save money. He turned part of his island into a resort in 1974, building thatched huts, bars and a dining hall for the expected flood of tourists, but not enough came, the elements refused to cooperate, and some half a million dollars evaporated into the Pacific night. The whole scheme, Brando admitted, had been "badly managed."

There was, of course, one obvious source of future capital—Brando's ability to command huge fees as a film actor. In this regard his views, as usual, were highly ambivalent. He had not changed his mind about the significance of movies or movie-acting. The latter, he told *Time* magazine, "is an empty and useless profession. I do it for the money because for me there is no pleasure . . . Movies? Forget it. I'm convinced that the larger the gross, the worse the picture. Bergman and Bunuel are visionaries, wonderful artists and craftsmen. How many people in the world have ever seen one of their films or ever heard of them? How can you take movies seriously?"

He depreciated his own recent successes with *The Godfather* and *Last Tango in Paris*. "Bertolucci was a very sensitive director, but I didn't like the movie. It was too calculated, designed to make an impact rather than a statement . . . *The Godfather*? What the hell did I know about a sixty-five-year-old Italian who smokes twisted goat-shit cigars?" He dismissed the idea that movies were influential in changing people's attitudes. "We're always going to change the world by communication, but it never quite works out, does it?" he told Bruce Cook. "We thought in the old days that radio would transform things—just get the message out to the people. Then it was the computers that stirred people's hopes and dreams. And what did the computers bring us?—Vietnam . . . What have the movies influenced? At least with television you know there is some direct influence. People buy air conditioners, automobiles, electric tweezers, because they've seen them advertised on television. But how do we use the machine? And how do we use movies? It seems to me there is some kind of pomposity to the idea that if we communicate these ideas people will listen, sparkles will come, and the cool breeze of truth will blow."

And if movies were so ineffective at stirring that breeze, then Brando must have felt extremely reluctant at the prospect of re-entering the world in which they were made, the world in which "the width of a Hollywood smile in my direction is commensurate with how my last picture grossed."

But he did need the money, and there's more than a suspicion that he only half-believed in the "emptiness" and "uselessness" of movies. Somewhere at the back of Brando's brain was a little voice which kept saying "movies can communicate some ideas, can have some influence, can at least ask relevant questions." He wasn't as certain as he often sounded. As he told someone on the set of his next film: "I can only state the facts as I see them. I'm for testing the mettle of your fundamental beliefs. How many of us do it? God knows, I don't enough. Sometimes I'm on my island and I wonder: what arena should I be in?"

When it came to one particular subject—the American Indian— he seemed in no doubt that an honest movie, one approved in advance by the American Indian Movement, could do nothing but good. He had been trying to get such a project off the ground for several years, and though his next major film, *The Missouri Breaks*, was not seen as a substitute for the Indian movie he had in mind, it does seem as if the two were connected. *The Missouri Breaks* would provide him with money which could be used to develop "his film," and, in itself, offered the possibility of a "serious study of the American Indian." Some hopes died hard.

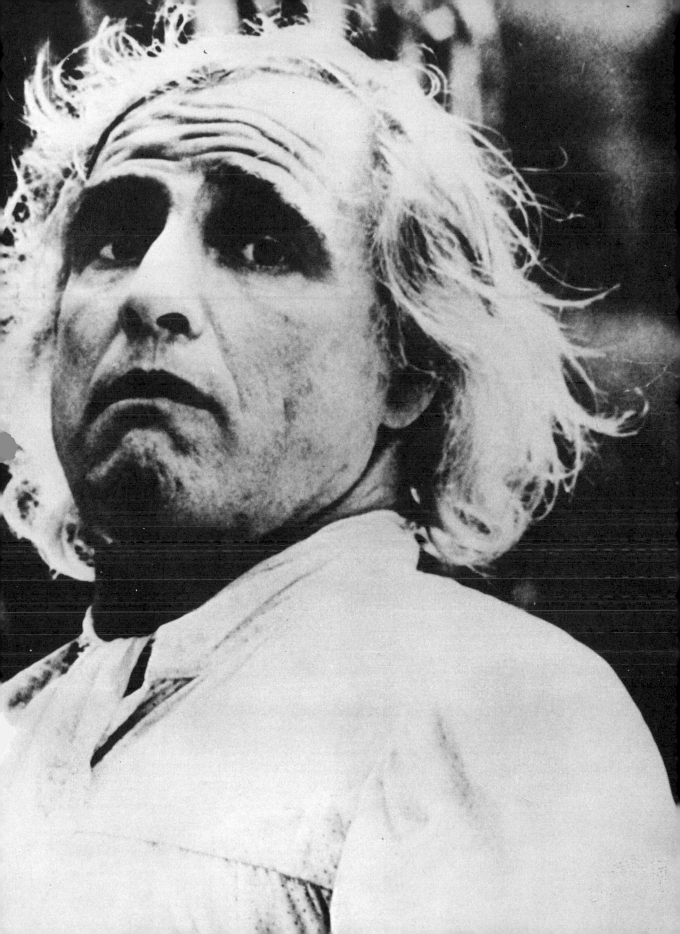

SHOOTING FISH

The Missouri Breaks opens with the hanging of a rustler. It may be illegal, it may be immoral, but like some contemporary pillars-of-the-community rancher David Braxton (John McLiam) has a misguided faith in the theory of deterrence. Just how misguided soon becomes apparent, as the dead man's colleagues are simply spurred to improve their own armory. A ranch of their own, they decide, will enable them to relay their ill-gotten horses more safely.

They rob a train to pay for said ranch, and while the rest of the gang head north for a cross-border raid on the stables of the Canadian Mounties, Logan (Jack Nicholson) sets about the task of looking like a real rancher. Braxton, true to the theory of deterrence, has meanwhile decided to up the stakes. He hires a "regulator," Lee Clayton (Brando), to solve the rustling problem once and for all. Clayton, like a nineteenth-century Pershing II, will only make things more dangerous for everybody.

While he spies on all and sundry, and particularly the suspicious Logan, through high-powered binoculars, Logan himself is becoming enamored of both the ranching life and Braxton's daughter Jane (Kathleen Lloyd).

His friends are now heading home from Canada, having successfully outwitted the Mounties. Clayton intercepts one of them, drowns him with some relish in a convenient river, and leaves his signature—a Sharps cartridge—in the headstall of the dead man's horse. When Logan learns of this he goes after Clayton, finds him defenseless in the Braxton bath, but cannot bring himself to shoot the chatty regulator in cold blood. He decided instead that the gang will steal all of Braxton's horses.

This they manage, but after splitting up for the purpose of selling the stolen mounts, they are picked off one by one by the seemingly ubiquitous Clayton. All, that is, except for Logan, whom Clayton mistakenly assumes has perished in a fire. He realizes his error rather abruptly, waking to hear Logan whisper: "Do you want to know what woke you? Lee, you've just had your throat cut."

Previous page:
Lee and his
favourite weapon

An ordinary enough plot perhaps. One that would not have looked out of place in a fifties "B" western. But within the basic plot-structure there's things going on which Audie Murphy never dreamed of. Right at the beginning the rustler who is about to die exchanges words with Braxton as they ride up the hill to the chosen tree. "It's a beautiful country," Braxton says. "Yes it is," the rustler replies. And once the noose is in place, the rancher courteously asks the condemned man whether he would like to set the horse in motion himself. "I will, sir," he says, and does. It's as if the whole story of *Easy Rider* has been told in a couple of minutes.

Returning to his ranch, Braxton argues with his daughter. He doesn't fulminate against rustling in moral terms; he's a businessman, he sees things in percentage terms. In this case, seven per cent of gross. Jane refuses to accept such terms, and through her "naivety" the corruption inherent in them is made apparent. And when he asks her to pass him down his copy of *Tristam Shandy,* corruption and culture are neatly tied together in one odious package.

The Missouri Breaks is a literate film, and at first glance seems full of literate characters. Clayton seems an astonishing creation, a burly, perfumed fop who kills people at half-mile range with his Creedmore rifle, and then pauses to admire the sunset. Brando's Fletcher Christian seems to have been cross-bred with Laughton's Captain Bligh. He thrives on his own eccentricities, talks a calculated mixture of whimsy and threat with any number of accents, and wears a bizarre range of costumes.

Logan is a more normative figure, one who develops with the film. Jane brings out and begins to ameliorate his fear of women, and looking after the ranch brings out his long-suppressed urge for a place of his own. She's much more than the usual romantic interest, stuck in the middle of a western to look good and to give the hero something to use and/or fall in love with. In fact she seems the most moral and the most intelligent character in the movie, a point not missed by Betsy Erkkila, who noted in *Cineaste* that the part constituted "a major breakthrough in women's roles in the American cinema."

It all sounds interesting, doesn't it? Two of America's most

Overleaf: Lee Clayton trying to look conventional

exciting actors, one of Hollywood's most lauded directors—
Arthur Penn—all working within a plot structure which seems
made for creative improvisation. Even a decent female role. What
could go wrong?

Quite a lot. *The Missouri Breaks,* although never less than
interesting, never becomes more than the sum of its parts.
Considering the intensity and political awareness which Brando,
Nicholson and Penn usually bring to their projects, it's amazing
how little of either they manage to generate together. And the
reasons for this failure are not hard to find—nearly all of them can
be traced to the way the project was put together, in the motivation
of the principals involved.

Nicholson wanted to work with Brando, with the actor "who
gave us our freedom." For Penn "it was Nicholson and Brando. I
just couldn't pass up a chance like that. You know, you make so few
movies in the course of your life, and so many of them have to do
with nursing actors through them, that when you get a chance like
this to go with two really superb heavyweights, why not go for
them, if for nothing else than to be present and participating in it.
That's why, in a sense, there is no thesis in this film. It was much
more an event. And it certainly shows, I think." One is reminded
of the music business in the early seventies, when certain
"supergroups" were formed whose prime reasons for existing
seemed to be a heartfelt love of mutual admiration and the mistaken
belief that you only had to bring talents together for sparks to fly.

It rarely worked for the musicians, and one of the main reasons
was the pressure of commercial realities. Everyone was so busy
being successful that there was never any time for such luxuries as
rehearsal, thought or a genuine meeting of the talents involved.
And so it was with *The Missouri Breaks.* The three principals found
a space in time when each would be free of other commitments,
and the fact that that space was only weeks away was deemed less
importance than the fact it existed at all. So there was no time for
adequate preparations, of script, costumes, locations, anything.
The suspicion persists that they were so sure of the power of their
combined talents that they felt they could get away with making a
film off the top of their heads.

Brando's wish to say something significant, to make the "serious study of the American Indian," was one of the first casualties. How he could ever have expected as much—there were, after all, no Indians in the story—only Brando could say, but in any case Penn soon put him right. "Gee, not at these prices," the director told the actor, who countered, "Arthur, at least let me have some fun."

And that's what you see—everyone having fun, displaying their literateness and intelligence in a film which never had a finalized shooting script, which rambles along as if tension was the last thing anyone had in mind. Nicholson is watchable—he always is—and Penn, after the event, wasd able to cobble together the thesis which he had earlier disclaimed. *The Missouri Breaks* was about "a phase of colonialism . . . the colonialists, in the form of Braxton, have been overthrown, leaving behind no real community, no political purpose." It was all "a metaphor for the modern world." And because most of his other films had been just that, had stored up enough coherent themes, the auteur industry was able to have as much fun with *The Missouri Breaks* as with the others. Like Penn's more recent *Night Moves,* the film represented an attempted "auto-destruction of generic codes," in the one case the private eye movie, in the other the western. Just as Gene Hackman played a pathetic, confused version of Marlowe, so Brando played a perverted version of the traditional law-enforcer. Clayton, according to Penn, was one of the "crazy ones," whom society calls forth to defend itself in the hour of its political degeneracy.

It sounds deep, the idea makes sense, but it's not something that you're likely to pick up from watching the movie. Brando's character has fascinating quirks, but he's not a fascinating character, and the actor knows it. "All these scenes in this movie have been seen 9,000 times before," he said on-set, "so it's essential to think of new things to try just to stay ahead of the audiences. Unconsciously, they know how the scene begins and what the actor will say. I've got to upset those expectations." And he did. Which was easy for someone with his talent and imagination. Like "shooting fish," he told Bruce Cook. Like fun.

There's no depth to Clayton, and that's the pity of *The Missouri Breaks.* Superficially he fits into the portrait gallery of establishment evil which the actor was now creating, but Clayton's ambivalences are all on the surface. A chance had been missed.

But who cared? Certainly not the producers, who knew that Nicholson and Brando together meant money whatever they chose to do. And not Brando, who would carry on saying that it was only a business anyway and that the money would be put to good use, which was true enough. Only the art of film would be ill-served, and for Brando the art of film was not of the contemporary world's most pressing issues.

CAMEOS

"My friends, you know me to be neither rash nor impulsive," says the voice of Brando. "I'm not given to wild unsupported statements," he continues. "Be reasonable," someone replies. "I've never been otherwise," Brando counters.

Where are we? Eavesdropping on some secret Hollywood tribunal? Ah, here's a clue. That's Trevor Howard telling him that "this discussion is terminated." This must be either an out-take from *Mutiny on the Bounty,* an early scene from *The Saboteur,* or an on-set disagreement during the making of either. But no, the discussion turns political. "You cannot ignore these facts," says Brando, "it's suicide . . . no, it's worse, it's genocide." The American Indian perhaps, or simply corporate civilization? "We must evacuate the planet immediately." Has he gone mad?

Of course, the visuals tell the real story. This is *Superman— The Movie,* and Brando is playing Superman's dad, the all-knowing Jorel, clued in to the imminent explosion of the planet Krypton. Like the real Brando he's facing an uphill task in getting anyone to see what's really going on.

Overleaf: Is it a bird? Is it a plane? No, it's a baby. With Susannah York and unnamed infant as the Superman family

It's doubtful whether the role's ironic undertones played any part in persuading the actor to take it. When you're offered something in the region of $4 million for around two week's work you don't need other reasons. *Superman* might be, as Brando said,

a "strictly commercial" undertaking, but it was definitely a superior commercial undertaking. Like the later *Flash Gordon* it had imagination and wit sprinkled among the special effects; it was built to be fun, and fun it was. The only real cause for regret lay in the rejection of Brando's suggestion that Jorel be dressed in a bagel.

He admitted he did it for the money. And "why not?" he added. "Money isn't the root of all evil—in the proper hands it can do a lot of good." In his hands it could be used for a project he had been developing with UNICEF and for research work on Tetiaroa. And there was no knowing how much of his own money he would need for the Indian film project.

This, in 1976, seemed on its way off the drawing-board. A script had been approved by Columbia, the Indian Movement was thought to be reasonably happy with it, and Brando himself was busy looking for a director. Perhaps he failed to find one; in any case the news was soon spreading that the film was off, and that a thirteen-part TV series was planned in its stead. Brando, it seems, had been much impressed by the similarly-motivated and highly successful series on American black history, *Roots.* He even asked to appear in the sequel, *Roots II,* and not with the fee in mind. He rang up Alex Haley, the series' author, told him how much he'd enjoyed the first series, and offered to take a minor role in the second. His only request was that it be a villainous role. The portrait gallery of evil would soon have another face.

Lincoln Rockwell, the American Nazi leader, was the chosen character, and for the first time in thirty years, Brando had an acting spot on TV. Only one scene was involved—Rockwell being interviewed by Haley for *Playboy* magazine—but it was a scene and a half. Brando sat behind the huge mahogany desk, framed by a portrait of Hitler and Nazi flags, radiating bigotry and paranoia. He received an Emmy award for those few minutes, and his fee was donated to charity. Interestingly enough, the scene was shot on Burbank's Stage 19, where *A Streetcar Named Desire* had been made a quarter-century before.

Both Jorel and Rockwell were cameos in the traditional sense, small parts played by a big name. The next cameo was of a different

As Nazi leader George Lincoln Rockwell in *Roots II*

order altogether, a small part only in terms of time onscreen: Colonel Kurtz dominates *Apocalypse Now* as surely as Don Corleone dominates *The Godfather*. He is the "heart of darkness," the psychological reality to which all the film's roads lead. As Willard (Martin Sheen) says at the beginning, talking of the trip awaiting himself and the audience: "I was going to the worst place in the world and I didn't even know it yet. Weeks away and hundreds of miles up a river that snaked through the war like a main circuit cable, plugged straight into Kurtz."

Apocalypse Now was a long time gestating. Its origins lay in pre-*Godfather* days: it was in 1969 that Coppola began work on a film centered around the American experience in Vietnam. At this stage he was set only to produce, with John Milius providing the script and George Lucas in the director's chair. But somehow the script wouldn't come right, and by the time another version was ready it seemed as though Milius himself would direct. This also fell through, leaving Coppola, now a huge success, in charge of all aspects of the project.

Casting consumed a few more years. Brando was the first and last choice for Kurtz, but the anchor-role of Willard was offered to and reputedly rejected by Steve McQueen, Al Pacino, James Caan and Jack Nicholson. Harvey Keitel took it, but didn't last long, and Sheen was eventually hired. At some point in this long process Gene Hackman, the first choice for Colonel Kilgore, gave way to Robert Duvall.

The filming was as drawn-out as the casting, consuming 238 days of location-shooting in the Philippines. Natural disasters were one reason—a typhoon in May 1976 destroyed sets and a huge quantity of equipment—but the movie-makers also generated their own extravagances. As Coppola put it: "We went insane. The film was made the way the war was fought. There were too many of us, too much money, too much equipment." The initial $12 million budget had reached nearly $30 million by completion.

It's not difficult to see where the money went: in the opening scene enough napalm is dropped on a stretch of jungle to keep the Ewings in business for a few months. This image is accompanied on the soundtrack by The Doors' "The End," and eventually the

Kurtz's lair in
Apocalypse Now

camera comes to rest on someone at the end of his tether, Captain Willard (Sheen), filling in the time between missions with nightmares in his Saigon hotel room.

Willard is an "unofficial" hit-man for the U.S. Army, and his sense of vocation is wearing thin. His and the film's first spoken words—"Saigon . . . shit"—seem to sum up the city, the war and his state of mind. He's just back from an unsatisfactory home leave—"I hardly said a word to my wife 'til I said yes to a divorce"—and another mission is the limit of his hopes. "And for my sins they gave me one."

Out in the jungle, across the Cambodian border, a renegade U.S. Colonel named Walter E. Kurtz (Brando) has set himself up as a local warlord, using his army of primitive Montagnard tribesmen to destroy anyone—Americans, North Vietnamese, Vietcong, South Vietnamese—who strays within reach. He's gone mad, the powers-that-be have decided, and Willard has been picked to "terminate his command," to terminate it "with extreme prejudice."

Willard catches the patrol boat that is to take him up the Nung River, meets the crew, "mostly just kids, rock'n'rollers with one foot in their graves." They sail down the coast to the river's mouth, and have trouble persuading the local air cavalry commander Colonel Kilgore (Duvall) to clear "Charlie" out of their path until one of his own men lets slip the intelligence that the Nung river-mouth is ideal for surfing. Other men insist that it's "real hairy in there," that it's "Charlie's point," but Kilgore has the ultimate answer to all and every such suggestion—"Charlie don't surf!" He sends his choppers in, blaring Wagner from the speakers and rocket-fire from the tubes, and after listening to a panegyric on the smell of napalm—"it smells like . . . victory"—Willard and the crew head on upriver.

The voyage continues, a series of set-pieces—A USO concert for the troops which gets out of hand, a fight over a bridge, a spear attack, a murderous encounter with a sampan full of Vietnamese civilians—interspersed with Willard's reading of the dossier on Walter E. Kurtz. Eventually they reach the latter's lair, and after a couple of enigmatic conversations Willard "successfully" fulfills his mission.

The plot, as a plot, is full of holes. Its overall shape, and some of the incidents and characterization, are taken from Conrad's novel *Heart of Darkness,* which describes a similar voyage up the Congo in the late nineteenth century. Kurtz's name and baldness, the spear attack, the words "the horror, the horror" which end the film, the images of indiscriminate shelling of the vast jungle, are all directly lifted from the original. So, for no logical rèason, is the journey by boat. Why, you might ask, doesn't Willard take a chopper like everyone else? And why, you might also ask, do the powers-that-be send Willard out on this mission alone? They've already sent one man, and he defected to Kurtz. They have no reason for thinking that Willard won't do the same; he's hardly the dependable type. And as for giving him an extensive dossier on Kurtz, which amounts in effect to a chance for Kurtz to argue his case—that seems like willful negligence.

While the film is proceeding upriver none of this matters very much, if at all. Coppola has captured, as he intended, the "sensuousness" of the war, and, as spectacle, Willard's journey through the madness is riveting. The quality of the narration, written by *Dispatches* author Michael Herr, more than compensates for any lapse in the visual impact. But once Willard reaches journey's end the film's problems come home to roost. The spectacle has been used to conceal the lack of logic, but when the boat and the film come to a halt in Kurtz' lair there is nothing big enough to hide the sudden lack of spectacle.

This is partly a "Hollywood problem," an inherent weakness of the chosen dramatic structure. The "Hollywood solution" would be to cap all that's gone before with a mind-numbing, eye-feasting attack on Kurtz's HQ, a visual apocalypse. Coppola reportedly shot such an ending, but for reasons that must be respected, declined to use it. He knew that such an ending would have turned the movie into nothing more than a celebration of madness, an "enjoy the spectacle of Vietnam in your plush theater seat" experience. He wanted the film to have more point than that; the end section had to go some way towards defining, reconciling, explaining all that preceded it.

What was the film supposed to be about? That was the problem, and there was only one character who could provide a solution—

Kurtz. All through the journey Willard muses on the question, and it's Kurtz who must supply the answers. "If that's how Kilgore fought the war," Willard reflects after the attack on the village, "I began to wonder what they had against Kurtz . . . it wasn't just insanity and murder; there was enough of that to go around for everyone."

The audience first hears Kurtz's voice on a taped radio broadcast during Willard's briefing for the mission. "I watched a snail crawl along the edge of a straight razor," the voice intones, "that's my dream, it's my nightmare: crawling along the edge of a straight razor, and surviving." Pretty enigmatic stuff, and the dossier isn't much more helpful. Kurtz had been one of the Army's brightest prospects, a general-in-the-making, an "humanitarian, a man of wit and humor." But he had taken his duties in Vietnam too seriously, and after he had ordered the assassination of four communist moles, his own Army had charged him with murder. He had defied them, turned renegade. His methods, according to his erstwhile superiors, had become "unsound."

A letter to his wife explains little more. Kurtz talks of "their" timid lying morality," and claims that ruthlessness is often nothing more than clarity. He shows some of the latter to the newly-arrived Willard, calling him "an errand boy sent by grocers to collect a bill," but soon thereafter reverts to being enigmatic. We hear him reciting Eliot's "The Hollow Men," a poem which expresses despair, disgust and not much else. His penultimate line—"We train our young men to rain fire on people but their commanders won't allow them to write 'fuck' on their airplanes because it's obscene"—though beautifully framed and delivered, expresses only the same disgust. This doesn't make him different: Willard has been saying much the same since he left the hotel room in Saigon. Kurtz, for all his way with parables, and for all that he's played by Marlon Brando, is nothing more than a Willard who's taken the final plunge, out of "the whole fucking program" and into a personal vision of hell which knows no personal limits.

There is no conclusion to *Apocalypse Now*. There are images of madness, the Kilgorian and the Kurtzian, and there are brutal, crushing reminders of the cost paid by less privileged humans. The

Kurtz, at the end of his military tether

sampan of innocent Vietnamese, slaughtered by Willard's "kids" in a paranoid outburst tells the story of this war in a few minutes. Even the gung-ho Kilgore, whom Willard ruefully guesses will escape without "so much as a scratch," is at some level a victim. No one escapes. No one can even go home. As Willard says: "I'd been

back there, and I knew that it just didn't exist anymore."

The war is everywhere. It explains Willard, Kilgore, Kurtz. But *Apocalypse Now* does not explain the war, does not even try to explain *this* war. Sol Yurick wondered in *Cineaste* why Coppola hadn't included scenes showing the decisions being made in Washington, and yes, that would have helped to set the story in its particular context. But Coppola wasn't really interested in the particular context, in the Vietnam war *per se*. That just happened to be a photogenic setting with a high emotional profile, somewhere to set *his* war. And *his* war is essentially a force of nature, self-generating, an aspect of the tragic human condition. The film's lack of conclusion is its own message, clear as crystal. We are the hollow men, we drop napalm on defenseless children, we achieve clarity only in our brutality. And there's nothing we can do about it.

"This is the end," sing the Doors, this is apocalypse now. The movie reflected the end of the seventies as perfectly as *Godfather/Tango* had reflected their beginning. Then the prevailing ideology of mainstream cinema had been disillusion, now expensive special effects cloaked in all-pervasive despair. Willard's journey was the ultimate con: sent to "the worst place in the world," he discovers that it's no different from anywhere else.

FORMULA THRILLER

With Francis Ford Coppola on the set of *Apocalypse Now*

The disappointment felt by many with regard to *Apocalypse Now* had much to do with the enormity of the expectations it had engendered. All the ballyhoo, the epic length of the production, the centrality of the subject-matter, the quality of the talents involved—all led people to expect more than could ever be delivered. If the questions which the film addressed were answerable in movie form, then the Vietcong would all have carried cameras.

Coppola noted that "Brando has been much more political

about this movie than I. He appreciates and understands the philosophical points, but he wanted me to hit nails on the head." Perhaps despair can be considered a philosophical position; certainly the film's picture of the war is a nail-hitting, not say head-banging, experience. The problem lay in the way the war got lost in the philosophy. Despair, when all's said and done, is a political nail you hit into your own head.

Brando's next film offered a different, more familiar version of themes in conflict, the story with political thrust eaten alive by the demands of a mundane Hollywood genre. *The Formula* was very much the brainchild of Steve Shagan, who wrote it, produced it and, eventually, re-edited it over the protests of director John Avildsen. The story follows private eye Barney Caine (George C. Scott) down a trail of murders and into a gigantic corporate conspiracy. The Nazis, it turns out, had hit on "the formula" for a fuel synthesized from coal, and cheaply to boot. Not unnaturally the oil companies, their inner offices replete with imaginary graphs of tumbling profits, have been moving heaven and earth to keep this formula secret until such time as they need to cash it in themselves. Unfortunately the secret keeps slipping out, hence the murders.

All of which offered three genres for the price of one film. The "Nazi legacy" leads into "the corporations are behind it all," which leads into the "private eye on the prowl." What more could an audience want?

Shagan thought Brando would make the perfect corporate boss, and the actor seemed to think so too. He liked the film's anti-corporate theme and he liked the idea of playing an overworld villain for the first time. He must have also been impressed with the money on offer—something in the region of $2 million for eleven days' work. He trusted Shagan and Avildsen, may well have admired their earlier, hard-hitting *Save the Tiger*. He checked into Santa Monica Hospital to shed excess weight and began thinking about the part of Adam Steiffel.

According to Shagan his first few ideas were unacceptable: Brando wanted the tycoon to live in an adobe hut in the desert tending lettuces—Corleone II—and to die of cheese asphyxiation. Perhaps he was trying it on; Shagan seems to have suspected as

A tycoon's breakfast for Adam Steiffel in *The Formula*

Overleaf: Steiffel reminds George C. Scott that 'Money, not morality, is the principal commerce of civilised nations' in *The Formula*

much, and encouraged him to think again. He did, with interesting results.

The plot takes George C. Scott from California to Berlin and back again, but there's not much point in going with him. Scott's as reliable as ever, Marthe Keller plays one more in a row of

assassinesses, and John Gielgud makes his obligatory appearance as an actor marooned in a movie. Brando has only three scenes but they all count. He's wearing a dental plate which stretches his mouth thin and wide, his hair's been mostly shaved off, he peers through rimless glasses and uses a hearing-aid. You don't get the impression, as with Don Corleone, that there's an animal within, in either the positive or negative sense. The sign on his wall in Shagan's novel—"When money talks, people listen"—sums up his view of his fellow man. Frogs are more important to him, and when one jumps into a chlorinated pool, he strains every sinew to rescue it. When his butler suggests Beethoven he pooh-poohs such taste, preferring to accompany a Benny Goodman record with drummers' brushes which he pulls from his dressing-gown pocket. This is the man responsible for the transatlantic trail of carnage which Scott is following. Like Corleone, he might say "nothing personal, it's just business," but unlike Corleone he has nothing personal to say. This is a godfather fit for the eighties.

Scott, after watching Brando perform, declared him "the greatest living actor. He has gone beyond the realm of acting. He creates like an impressionist painter." Unfortunately the critics were less impressed by either Brando or the movie. The charge that the story was incomprehensible was unfounded, but most of the other criticisms were not. The script was mostly awful, and the dreadful conventions of the "international thriller"—lots of scenic travel, a heroine regardless of the need for one, many and varied deaths—all combined to create a deadening sense of déjà vu. Not enough time and imagination had been spent, and a sound idea had been put to shoddy use. *The Formula* ended up justifying its title and not much else.

BUT IS IT ART?

"It may seem peculiar," Brando told a reporter in the mid-sixties, "but I've spent most of my career wondering what I'd like to do.

Of course, I've had to make a living, to support children and wives, but I have a variety of interests—reading, traveling, meeting people—which have been as important a part of my life as working as an actor. Perhaps it's hard for people to understand, but acting has never been the dominant factor in my life . . ."

By the beginning of the eighties it hardly seemed a factor at all. He was scheduled to appear in *Superman II,* and was reportedly paid $1.5 million for a week's work on the project, but when the cast list was released his name was conspicuous by its absence. Some say the producers belatedly decided they couldn't afford him, some that the storyline was changed for other reasons, but either way, Superman's dad was left mouldering on Krypton.

In 1980 he was allegedly offered his biggest ever fee to take the lead in a big-budget Hollywood version of Pablo Picasso's life. Since Brando had himself dubbed Picasso the last real artist, there was every expectation that he would regard such a project sympathetically. Perhaps the script was appalling, perhaps he just didn't feel like making a movie, but nothing has emerged in the several years since.

His personal life has been subject to the usual press comment. A large circulation British newspaper reported all sorts of ailments for which he has ostensibly been treated. In interviews he has sounded more benign of late, looking back on his life with something approaching vague amusement. "Four kids by three different women," he reflects. "I had a real Ford assembly line going throughout much of my life. If you're rich and famous, getting laid a lot isn't difficult. I knew what I was doing, but I didn't know why I was doing it. I still don't have all the answers." He was ready to accept that his attitude to women had not been, in retrospect, all that he would have liked it to be. "We've all been guilty, most men, of viewing women through prejudice. I always thought of myself not as a prejudiced person, but I find, as I look over it, that I was."

At last he and Tarita had remained friends and partners in child-rearing after the end of their sexual relationship, and his love-affair with the South Seas seems unlikely ever to abate. The famous beach hut is being replaced by a modern luxury building, complete with aquarium, solar heating and the best radio equipment. Brando is a dedicated radio ham, and listeners around the world who tune in for a chat with "Marcos" might recognize something familiar in his voice.

He doesn't live full-time on Tetiaroa, and his career as a political figure continues. He's now been involved with UNICEF for more than twenty years, and has every reason to be proud of the effort he's put in. He's not, of course, preferring to discuss his involvement in matter-of-fact terms: "We've put on shows in Paris, London, Japan, the U.S., traveled around the world, done promos . . . Mainly, my task has been trying to communicate what UNICEF has done, how much the world needs UNICEF, and what a valuable investment children are . . ." He's probably still trying to get the Indian series off the ground, and the notion of using Tetiaroa as a testing-ground for futures that work has not been abandoned. Does he think he's been successful in getting the various messages across?—"I've no way of knowing. I have always done my best, but there's always a sense of failure because there is always so much to do."

The loner, the father and the politician leave little time for the film star. It doesn't concern him unduly. "I'm not guilty about not working—in films—more, because I've shed that puritan superficiality. What I do, I try to do well, and I feel quality is more significant than quantity. I don't try to do a movie every so often, but just when something comes along that's of interest or pays a lot of money when I'm in need of funds."

Perhaps his movie-career is virtually over; it's hard to escape the feeling that a sustained series of full-blooded performances is now out of the question. It is, after all, more than a decade since his last full-length role in *Tango,* and there's been no sign in the intervening period that he hungers, as an actor, for characters. For the money and what the film might say, occasionally. But not for the joy of acting.

He's made thirty-one films in his career, and though many could match the quantity there's none who could match the quality. He's simply made more great films than anyone else. A stray visitor from Krypton seeking to understand the changes that have taken place in the post-war period could do a lot worse than sit through *Streetcar, The Wild One, Waterfront, One-Eyed Jacks, The Chase,*

Reflections in a Golden Eye, Queimada, The Godfather, Last Tango and *Apocalypse Now*. For those of us who've been stuck on Earth during the period in question such films have made the cinema worthwhile, entertaining as they challenged, challenging as they entertained.

Even the bad films—and there have been remarkably few of them—have been worth watching for Brando's performance alone. He's never been easy to criticize as an actor, as even those most involved in professional disagreements with him have testified. Kubrick, for instance, must have left *One-Eyed Jacks* feeling more than a little peeved, but soon he was telling James Mason of Brando's great theatrical intelligence, of how he could improvise entire plot developments and impressive exchanges of dialogue on the spur of the moment.

But Brando has always been more than a great actor, and fellow-actor Louis Jourdan summed up one aspect of his importance with the phrase "the Don Quixote of actors." Brando was "always tilting at the system," he was "revenge for us all, for all the injustices we actors have to put up with." This can be expanded beyond Jourdan's meaning, for Brando has often seemed a Don Quixote of the contemporary world, tilting at targets that many thought were none of an actor's business. He has always known that they're everyone's business, he's taken the time to know what he's talking about, and he's never been slow to put his money where his mouth is. The political columnist James Wechsler, who met him at the height of the sixties, said that "there are few people with whom I have conversed who seem to know—and care—as much as Brando does about the quest for human dignity in which we are now engaged."

To some extent Brando's successes as an actor and as a political figure have not been successfully merged in his film career. This was particularly true during the sixties. But the ten films listed above show just how much success has been achieved; there can be little doubt that he is one of the most significant artistic figures of the post-war world.

He would of course deny this. "In your heart of hearts," he told a *Playboy* interviewer, "you know perfectly well that movie stars aren't artists . . . I don't know of any movie actors, or actors . . . there are *no* people . . . We can call them artists, give them the generic term if they're comfortable with that, but in terms of great art—magnificent art, art that changes history, art that's overwhelming—where are they? Where are the great artists today? Name one. When you look at Rembrandt or Baudelaire or listen to the Discourses of Epictetus, you know the quality of men is not the same. There are no giants today. Mao Tse-tung was the last giant."

Today's artists were something else entirely. "We've somehow substituted craft for art and cleverness for craft. It's revolting! It's *disgusting* that people talk about art and they haven't got the right to use the word. It doesn't belong on anyone's tongue in this century. There are no artists. We are businessmen. We're merchants. There is no art."

There's some truth in all this, quite a lot of truth, and at one level it's easy to respect Brando for wanting to put his own achievements in perspective. When he says that "compared to world affairs, to peace conferences, making a movie is absolutely nothing," it's easier to agree than disagree. But at another level it does seem as if familiarity with the movie-world has bred a contempt which is too all-embracing. Movies will continue to be made, and it *is* important that as many as possible—as many as their being a business allows—are entertaining, thought-provoking, conducive to the spread of that human understanding which the younger Brando sought to encourage. He himself said, in another context, that "everything passes, nothing lasts for more than a short while," but the better movies do last, just as Baudeliare, Rembrandt and Epictetus have lasted. The commercial pressures on art are heavier than ever, and it is right to say so, but when it comes to artists as changers of history, who but Marlon Brando would consider Baudeliare a more influential figure than himself?

Rarely for the times, he has been an actor without a unidimensional image; he has reflected change as he sought to promote it. Fashions, like fashion itself, are a way of channelling creativity into non-critical—in both senses of the word—activity; Brando has never been fashionable. His creativity has constantly

been put to critical use, and that's art, whether he likes it or not.
"Where are the great artists today? Name one."
OK. Marlon Brando.

FILMOGRAPHY

THE MEN (1950)
Director: Fred Zinnemann. Screenplay: Carl Foreman. Producer: Stanley Kramer. Co-stars: Teresa Wright, Everett Sloan. Character: Ken Wilozek.

A STREETCARD NAMED DESIRE (1951)
Director: Elia Kazan. Screenplay: Tennessee Williams, from his own play, adapted by Oscar Saul. Producer: Charles K. Feldman. Co-stars: Vivien Leigh, Kim Hunter, Karl Malden. Character: Stanley Kowalski.

VIVA ZAPATA! (1952)
Director: Elia Kazan. Screenplay: John Steinbeck, from Edgcomb Pichon's *Zapata the Unconquerable.* Producer: Darryl F. Zanuck. Co-stars: Anthony Quinn, Jean Peters, Joseph Wiseman. Character: Emiliano Zapata.

JULIUS CAESAR (1953)
Director: Joseph L. Mankiewicz. Screenplay: William Shakespeare. Producer: John Houseman. Co-stars: James Mason, John Gielgud, Edmund O'Brien, Louis Calhern, Greer Garson, Deborah Kerr. Character: Mark Antony.

THE WILD ONE (1953)
Director: Lazlo Benedek. Screenplay: John Paxton, from story by Frank Rooney. Producer: Stanley Kramer. Co-stars: Mary Murphy, Robert Keith, Lee Marvin. Character: Johnny.

ON THE WATERFRONT (1954)
Director: Elia Kazan. Screenplay: Budd Schulberg, suggested by articles by Malcolm Johnson. Producer: Sam Spiegel. Co-stars: Eva Marie Saint, Karl Malden, Lee J. Cobb, Rod Steiger. Character: Terry Malloy.

DESIRÉE (1954)

Director: Henry Koster. Screenplay: Daniel Taradash, from Annemarie Selinko's novel. Producer: Julius Blaustein. Co-stars: Jean Simmons, Merle Oberon, Michael Rennie, Cameron Mitchell. Character: Napoleon Bonaparte.

GUYS AND DOLLS (1955)

Director: Joseph L. Mankiewicz. Screenplay: Joseph L. Mankiewicz, from play with book by Jo Sterling and Abe Burrows, in turn from story by Damon Runyon. Producer: Sam Goldwyn. Co-stars: Jean Simmons, Frank Sinatra, Vivian Blaine. Character: Sky Masterson.

THE TEAHOUSE OF THE AUGUST MOON (1956)

Director: Daniel Mann. Screenplay: John Patrick, from own play, based on novel by Vern Sneider. Producer: Jack Cummings. Co-stars: Glenn Ford, Machiko Kyo, Eddie Albert, Paul Ford. Character: Sakini.

SAYONARA (1957)

Director: Joshua Logan. Screenplay: Paul Osborn, from novel by James A. Michener. Producer: William Goetz. Co-stars: Miiko Taka, Red Buttons, Patricia Owens. Character: Major Lloyd Gruver.

THE YOUNG LIONS (1958)

Director: Edward Dymtryk. Screenplay: Edward Anhalt, from novel by Irwin Shaw. Producer: Al Lichtman. Co-stars: Montgomery Clift, Dean Martin, Hope Lange, Barbara Rush, May Britt, Maximilian Schell. Character: Christian Diestl.

THE FUGITIVE KIND (1960)

Director: Sidney Lumet. Screenplay: Tennessee Williams and Meade Roberts, from former's play *Orpheus Descending*. Producers' Martin Jurow, Richard A. Shepherd. Co-stars: Anna Magnani, Joanne Woodward, Maureen Stapleton, Victor Jory. Character: Val Xavier.

ONE-EYED JACKS (1961)

Director: Marlon Brando. Screenplay: Guy Trosper and Calder Willingham, from Charles Neider's novel *The Authentic Death of Hendry Jones*. Co-stars: Karl Malden, Pina Pellicer, Katy Jurado, Ben Johnson, Slim Pickens, Larry Duran. Character: Rio.

MUTINY ON THE BOUNTY (1962)

Director: Lewis Milestone. Screenplay: Charles Lederer, from novel trilogy by Charles Nordhoff and James Norman Hall. Producer: Aaron Rosenberg. Co-stars: Trevor Howard, Richard Harris. Character: Fletcher Christian.

THE UGLY AMERICAN (1963)

Director: George Englund: Screenplay: Stewart Stern, from novel by William J. Lederer and Eugene Burdick. Producer: George Englund. Co-stars: Eija Okada, Sandra Church, Pat Hingle. Character: Harrison Carter MacWhite.

BEDTIME STORY (1964)

Director: Ralph Levy. Screenplay: Stanley Shapiro, Paul Henning. Producer: Stanley Shapiro. Co-stars: David Niven, Shirley Jones. Character: Fred Benson.

THE SABOTEUR: CODE NAME—MORITURI (1965)

Director: Bernhard Wicki. Screenplay: Daniel Taradsh, from novel by Werner Jörg Lüdecke. Producer: Aaron Rosenberg. Co-stars: Yul Brynner, Trevor Howard, Janet Margolin. Character: Robert Crain.

THE CHASE (1966)

Director: Arthur Penn. Screenplay: Lillian Hellman, from Horton Foote's play and novel. Producer: Sam Spiegel. Co-stars: Jane Fonda, Robert Redford, James Fox, E. G. Marshall, Angie Dickinson. Character: Sheriff Calder.

THE APPALOOSA (1966) (SOUTHWEST TO SONORA in UK)

Director: Sidney J. Furie. Screenplay: James Bridges and Roland Kibbee, from novel by Robert MacLeod. Producer: Alan Miller. Co-stars: John Saxon, Anjanette Comer. Character: Matt.

A COUNTESS FROM HONG KONG (1967)

Director: Charles Chaplin. Screenplay: Charles Chaplin. Producer: Jerome Epstein. Co-stars: Sophia Loren, Sydney Chaplin, Tippi Hedren. Character: Ogden.

REFLECTIONS IN A GOLDEN EYE (1967)

Director: John Huston. Screenplay: Chapman Mortimer, Gladys Hill, from novel by Carson McCullers. Producer: Ray Stark. Co-stars: Elizabeth Taylor, Brian Keith, Julie Harris, Robert Forster, Zorro David. Character: Major Weldon Pemberton.

CANDY (1968)

Director: Christian Marquand. Screenplay: Buck Henry, from novel by Terry Southern and Mason Hoffenberg. Producer: Robert Haggiag. Co-stars: Ewa Aulin, Richard Burton, James Coburn, Walter Matthau, Charles Aznavour, etc. Character: Grindl.

THE NIGHT OF THE FOLLOWING DAY (1969)

Director: Hubert Cornfield. Screenplay: Hubert Cornfield, Robert Phippeny, from Lionel White's novel *The Snatchers*. Producer: Hubert Cornfield. Co-stars: Richard Boone, Rita Moreno, Pamela Franklin, Jess Hahn. Character: Bud.

QUEIMADA! (1970) (BURN in U.S.)

Director: Gillo Pontecorvo. Screenplay: Franco Solinas, Giorgio Arlorio, from story they wrote with Pontecorvo. Producer: Alberto Grimaldi. Co-stars: Evaristo Marquez, Renato Salvatore. Character: Sir William Walker.

THE NIGHTCOMERS (1971)

Director: Michael Winner. Screenplay: Michael Hastings, using characters created by Henry James. Producer: Michael Winner. Co-stars: Stephanie Beacham, Thora Hird. Character: Peter Quint.

THE GODFATHER (1972)

Director: Francis Ford Coppola. Screenplay: Francis Ford Coppola and Mario Puzo, from latter's novel. Producer: Albert S. Ruddy. Co-stars: James Caan, Al Pacino, Robert Duvall, Diane Keaton, Richard Castellano, Sterling Hayden, Richard Conte, Al Lettieri. Character: Don Vito Corleone.

LAST TANGO IN PARIS (1972)

Director: Bernardo Bertolucci. Screenplay: Franco Arcalli, Bernardo Bertolucci. Producer: Alberto Grimaldi. Co-star: Maria Schneider. Character: Paul.

THE MISSOURI BREAKS (1976)

Director: Arthur Penn. Screenplay: Thomas McGuane. Producer: Robert Sherman. Co-stars: Jack Nicholson, Kathleen Lloyd, Randy Quaid, Frederick Forrest, Harry Dean Stanton, John McLiam. Character: Lee Clayton.

SUPERMAN—THE MOVIE (1978)

Director: Richard Donner. Screenplay: Mario Puzo, David Newman, Robert Benton, Leslie Newman. Producer: John Barry. Co-stars: Christopher Reeve, Margot Kidder, Gene Hackman, Valerie Perrine, Jackie Cooper, Trevor Howard, Susannah York, Phyllis Thaxter, Glenn Ford, Ned Beatty. Character: Jorel.

APOCALYPSE NOW (1979)

Director: Francis Ford Coppola. Screenplay: Francis Ford Coppola, John Milius. Producer: Francis Ford Coppola. Co-stars: Martin Sheen, Robert Duvall. Character: Kurtz.

THE FORMULA (1980)

Director: John G. Avildsen. Screenplay: Steve Shagan. Producer: Steve Shagan. Co-stars: George C. Scott, Marthe Keller. Character: Adam Steiffel.

INDEX